EVEn more
Adventures in Retirement

EVEn more
Adventures in Retirement

Eve Day

ISIS
LARGE PRINT
Oxford

First published in Great Britain 2008
by
Eve Day

Published in Large Print 2009 by ISIS Publishing Ltd.,
7 Centremead, Osney Mead, Oxford OX2 0ES
by arrangement with
Author

British Library Cataloguing in Publication Data
Day, Eve.
EVEn more [text (large print)]: adventures in
retirement. - - (Reminiscence)
1. Day, Eve - - Travel.
2. Day, Eve - - Family.
3. Retired women - - Travel.
4. Retired women - - Biography.
5. Voyages and travels.
6. Large type books.
I. Title II. Series
910.4'092–dc22

ISBN 978–0–7531–8358–8 (hb)
ISBN 978–0–7531–8359–5 (pb)

Printed and bound in Great Britain by
T. J. International Ltd., Padstow, Cornwall

They call me the "Limerick Queen"
On rhyming I've always been keen
If you take a look
I have scattered this book
With a few of them, most of them clean.

Dedicated to all those I love and have loved

Time is nature's way of stopping everything
happening at once.

Sincere thanks to good friends Krysia Stafford and Anne Walsh for all their support and advice.

Contents

Foreword

Here once again are more interesting and colourful adventures of Eve for you to enjoy. I am sure those of you who have read the first three books will really be looking forward to this one. I find it incredible that she remembers it all in such detail!

This book tells mainly of her amazing travels from one end of the globe to the other. One thing I have to say about Eve, is that she is an inspiration, having such a great sense of courage and adventure, sometimes in the face of adversity. I put this down to her wicked sense of humour and her ability to see the ridiculous side of any situation.

There is also deep sadness in this book which tells of the tragic loss of her dear and only son Oliver. When I first met Eve, I was newly wed and a very new pre-school teacher at Armadale Kindergarten way back in 1972. She was busy with her young family of three. How could either of us know in those happy days, that we were both to lose our only sons in the prime of their lives and both in tragic circumstances? A bond neither of us would choose at any price! We worked together for four enjoyable years and have been great friends ever since. Eve has always been a person whom I have admired because in spite of everything life has dealt her, she has always picked herself up and 'just got on with things', participating in numerous activities, social events and adventures and has had an extremely full and eventful life. She literally never lets the grass grow under her feet.

As limericks appeal to Eve, I thought I would make an attempt to write one for her.

(Not her standard but the best I could do!)

Young at Heart — for Eve.
"There was a 'young' lady named Eve
Who carries her heart on her sleeve.
Kids vote her the best
When she's put to the test,
And so do we all, I believe!"

The last book *EVEntually*, Concluding the memories of Adamant Eve was meant to be the last, and now this one is once again meant to be the last. However . . . knowing Eve as I do, something tells me that she still has a lot of adventuring to do!!

Read and enjoy.

Krysia Stafford

CHAPTER
ONE

Retirement 1995

I've had a happy working life, retirement has begun.
I've fitness, faculties, freedom, finance,
now I'll have some fun.

Retirement at last!

I had ambivalent feelings about it for the final few months working as an assistant at Kelmscott Pre-Primary School.

I had been there for twenty happy years but at sixty five I felt ready for a change of direction in my life.

It took only six weeks before I said "Hey, I like this." I was certainly ready physically and emotionally for whatever lay ahead.

I realise that it is nearly forty years since we emigrated to Western Australia from England and that I had been here over half my life.

I have been very fortunate that Don was never without employment. He admitted after his retirement that he had always enjoyed his work and had never once got up in the morning thinking "Ugh, work today."

He has always been very generous and my wages just helped with extras. Because of this, and the various jobs I held concurrently, I was able to save for my retirement. I remembered the old song, "I've got sixpence".

"Tuppence to spend and tuppence to lend and tuppence to send home to my wife."

I always tried to use a bit of discipline with my money and save one third.

My ambitions were to live by "F" words. As long as I had my fitness, faculties, freedom and finance then I'll have *fun*.

Fun is what you make it.

Don retired many years before me.

He never cared about socialising.

His main interests are solitary, reading and gardening.

Gradually he took over the shopping as it gave him an outing every day. As he had plenty of time whilst I was still working, and enjoyed it, (also he says in self-defence,) he cooked the main meal.

He had always made the decisions about our menus and now was happily in total control. This gave me not only the freedom to participate in my various and varied activities but also the comfort of knowing that he is able to cope happily if I am not there.

Initially I said I had three ambitions when I retired, to visit Ireland, to visit Tasmania, and to go up in a hot air balloon, not necessarily in that order.

I will tell how I achieved these dreams within the first few years.

I have had so many other adventures and achievements that I am constantly surprised and delighted with the unpredictability of life.

Rhyme I wrote for Les Guthrie the Headmaster, the month after I retired.

I should have written earlier, at least I really
    meant to.
I've had birthday celebrations and I do apologize.
I certainly appreciate the trouble that you went
    to.
The authorised certificate was such a big
    surprise.
Clare's speech at the Assembly was such a big
    event, too.
The large bouquet of flowers brought teardrops
    to my eyes.
Please thank all the teachers for their gift. I will
    comment too
On the kind words in the card, as they wished
    me their *goodbyes*.
— A sybaritic life for me. Now I'll be content to
Enjoy my many interests. It's great to realise.
Thank you for your kind words and wishes that
    you sent, too.
It's been a happy twenty years. My goodness,
    how time flies!

CHAPTER
TWO

Epitaph for grandmother 1996

A lovely time in Scotland but Rome was purgatory.
Discover mother's grave and meet ancient cousin "Gee".

The first year after I retired I had a quite adventurous holiday.

I had spent twenty seven happy years in Armadale, near Perth in Western Australia but I am incorrigibly nostalgic, and knew I wanted to see England and many of my dear friends and relations again.

Initially I stayed with my nephew Jack, his wife Ginny and children Alister and Anabel. She was an entrancing little girl and although only four, passionate about dancing. I remember her standing in front of the television, watching a recording of the Irish company, "Riverdance." She imitated the steps perfectly and very seriously. Derek, Jack's brother was also staying there from New Zealand, with his little girl Rayna. We all visited dear cousin Marcelle for her ninetieth birthday and took her to Battersea Park for a picnic. This amazing lady and very dear friend, had wonderful stamina and could have out-walked me, even then.

I had booked a weekend at The Old Rectory in Fittleworth, Sussex.

This charming very old building had been extended and was now used as an Adult Residential Learning Centre.

The well qualified chef cooked excellent meals and they held a large variety of courses there throughout the year.

Whilst I was there, three courses were running. Stock market for beginners, the Annual Miniature Painters seminar, (No, not for midgets!) and Aromatherapy.

Only two of us were enrolled for this and they kindly did not cancel it, as I had come from Australia to participate.

Pam and I had a great time, as we were so compatible and our teacher Janet was fun too.

Pam had her car there and on our free afternoon took me to Arundel for a few hours, always a favourite town of mine. What a treat! I remember Veronica when she was very small, looking at the lovely castle and saying,

"I know who lives there. It is the 'Norf of Dufolk'!" A lovely spoonerism.

That day this charming ancient town even had the Town Crier walking around ringing his bell. I was thrilled to see such a typical English icon.

On Sunday I visited the adjacent church at Fittleworth, part of which dated from Saxon times, so was probably about a thousand years old, incredible!

The graveyard was equally interesting in a very tranquil setting with yew trees and fascinating, well worn inscriptions.

During the weekend I was interrogated.

"Tell me 'Australia', My title, from a dear little 'miniature' lady. (Tautology?) Are there birds where you live?"

She lived alone in a small village in Suffolk and had little knowledge of the outside world. Travelling to Sussex had been an enormous adventure for her.

This interesting weekend was enhanced by Pam taking me to visit her lovely home in nearby Horsham to admire the exquisite dolls house she was furnishing.

Afterwards I returned to Jack's home in Twickenham.

There was a young lady of Twickenham
Whose shoes were too tight to walk quick in 'em.
She came back from a walk
Looking whiter than chalk,
And took 'em both off and was sick in 'em.

I had a very moving afternoon with dear family friend Basil. We had tea near Kew Gardens in the Tea Rooms that made the original "maid of honour" cakes and still specialises in them.

He then drove me to Willesden Jewish Cemetery to show me where my mother had been buried, as I had no idea. She is not individually named but is in the large Rosenbaum family grave.

The inscription my grandfather wrote for his wife, brought tears to my eyes.

**"In ever loving memory of Leah for 45 years
the wife, sweetheart and inseparable companion
of Jack Rosenbaum of 12 Hinde Street W.1.
who passed away on April 21st 1924. Third day
of Passover 5684 in her 67th year.
The devoted mother of Charles, Joel, Harry,
Edgar, Flora, Queene.
Charitable in thought and action with the heart
and soul of an angel. She only did what she
thought was right."**

Basil also had a huge treat for me. He had managed to get tickets for the Opera at Glyndebourne. This very prestigious venue is owned privately.

The Opera season is just for a few months in the summer.

It is compulsory for the men to wear dinner jackets, trousers and bow ties and the ladies, long dresses. Basil had forewarned me.

Handel's "Theodora" has a very grim story. This unusual production was portrayed in modern dress. The heroine's death by lethal injection, was prolonged by the never-ending arias. Still, it was a memorable experience.

Basil had booked us a very nice meal in the restaurant there. Afterwards, we wandered through the immaculate grounds. Here people had set up elaborate, sophisticated picnics with white cloths and candelabra on the tables, an unforgettable sight.

It was after midnight when Basil returned me to Jack's home. He lived not far away in Richmond.

I then went to Great Bookham in Surrey where I spent a few days with my dear friend Veronica, my godmother "Diddley's" eldest daughter. I am godmother to her second son James and she took me to visit him and his partner in a village some distance away.

"He lives in Sandy Lane" she said.

"Oh," I replied "I used to live in a Sandy Lane in 1940."

There must be dozens of Sandy Lanes in Surrey.

Eventually we saw the road sign and drove towards his home. It is no longer a sandy lane but a made-up road and it suddenly brought back vivid memories. I was sure this was the same road.

We chatted to James' elderly neighbour and yes, the Hoy family with whom I had stayed, had lived next door but one. What a coincidence. I had not known earlier, as the village boundaries had changed and this was now named Churt, not Tilford.

Sid, our best man and his wife Rita live in Walthamstow and I stayed with them for a few days. We spent one morning exploring all the delights of the High Street.

This street market , founded in 1885, is over a mile long and has over 500 stalls. Although one sees many different ethnic participants and customers, it still has a predominantly Cockney atmosphere. There is a huge choice of merchandise, anything from fresh eels in tanks, to ladies knickers.

"Come on darlin', only two quid fer five pairs, give yer ole man a treat."

Another day we visited the William Morris Gallery in Lloyd Park. This lovely old building was put to a different use during the war and Don remembers visiting the dentist there.

Sid and Rita's home is near Epping Forest and on my final evening we went to "Ye Old King's Head" for a meal. This charming old inn originated in the 15th century.

I then caught the train to Taunton in Somerset where dear friend Ronnie met me and drove me to their farm at nearby Wrantage. Doug, her husband, spent all his time and energy converting one of the old barns into a dwelling.

Meanwhile, we went sightseeing in this very attractive area and enjoyed the gardens and house of Knightshayes, an impressive Victorian gothic mansion. We ascended to the second floor in the tiniest lift I have ever seen.

We also drove to Cricket St Thomas. This appealing village was the venue of the television series "To the Manor Born", many of the scenes being filmed in the Manor house there, but this was not open to the public.

Chris their eldest daughter invited Ronnie and me to stay with her and Ray in their exquisite cottage in Berkshire. We happened to drive across the country on June 21st, the day of the summer solstice. We were delayed, as the traffic was dense around Stonehenge because of the sightseers and revellers joining the Druids to celebrate the longest day of the year.

We lunched at a town that has umpteen antique shops both sides of the road. This irresistible attraction

9

delayed us further. We arrived to a very warm welcome and I admired their home where everything was colour co-ordinated and immaculate, even the garden.

During our few days stay we went to Disraeli's home at Hughenden Manor, a huge house with spectacular gardens. We enjoyed the traditional cottages of the Cotswold villages and also some of the prosperous Thames-side towns such as Marlow.

My next hosts were Margaret and Douglas in Wickford Essex, our old neighbours and good friends. They always made me so welcome.

Wickford is where we lived for some years before emigrating.

Hyde Hall belonging to the Royal Horticultural Society is only a couple of miles away. Don would have loved the huge and varied display of roses. He and Douglas were both keen gardeners. The exhibits and variety were quite breathtaking in this lovely setting. The acres of colour were absolutely stunning.

I took the opportunity to meet up with a few old friends. I used to run a group for small children with various handicaps.

It was an excellent job to return to with a family, as I was able to take two year old Oliver with me and also the girls during their holidays. It gave them an early understanding and empathy towards children with disabilities.

One little boy who attended had no obvious handicap but was unable to play naturally at home as his elder brother was autistic.

I had always stayed in touch with them each Christmas, so now visited them. Ian was married but Clive of course was still at home. He attended a Day Centre and was reasonably socialised. His speech was like a robot, completely without any expression. His father told me that Clive was helping him dig in the garden recently, when he had to go inside to answer the phone. Clive knew how to follow commands and had been told to dig. When his father returned, he thought he must have had almost dug through to Australia!

Alison, with whom I was friendly when I had her little boy at Pre-School in Australia a few years previously, was helping me to learn spoken Italian. She too was in England visiting her parents with her two children, aged nine and eleven.

We had decided to have a brief visit to Italy together. After the flight to Rome, a friend of Alison's met us and took us to visit Ostia Antica on the outskirts of the city.

Most of the interesting archaeological remains are from the Third Century B.C. We saw ruins of temples, an amphitheatre and some beautiful mosaics. We stayed at a hotel in Central Rome.

I had hoped we would visit some places of interest before heading for Naples but both children were fractious and didn't like walking or sightseeing. Most of all they objected strongly and loudly to travelling on the crowded Naples-bound train.

"We're getting off."

I staggered off the packed train with my suitcase to join them on the platform. They were red faced with anger and Alison told me they were all returning to England straight away, I could do what I wished.

I was flabbergasted.

My knowledge of the language was minimal and I would never have stayed there alone, so I reluctantly flew back to Heathrow that evening too.

An extremely kind gentleman from Folkestone sat next to me and could see I was distressed. He took me under his capable wing.

We arrived at Heathrow and I saw Alison and the children gaping at me with this handsome stranger.

Robin had his couriered car waiting, whisked me to a nearby hotel, gave me a chaste kiss on the cheek and was off. What a knight in shining armour to help a "damsel" (some damsel!) in such distress.

He had told me he was a member of the Lions Club and I eventually located him via another Club and was able to write and thank him for his gallantry.

This unexpected hotel stay saw me frantically phoning Maureen, my dear school friend, who I was not due to visit until a week later.

Bless her, she and Paddy were able to meet me in Oxford the following afternoon. I was so disappointed in the abortive Italian trip as I had been really looking forward to it. Still, it was a relief and a blessing to have such good friends.

Maureen and Paddy had recently retired to a small village in Worcestershire. Their beautifully renovated barn provided four bedrooms and roomy living areas.

They seemed happily settled.

One day Maureen kindly took me for a half hour's drive to Wyre Piddle, a real picture book village, where my cousin Gladys and husband Alec lived.

I had not seen them since my marriage.

Now ninety seven and a half and considerably shrunken in stature, her spirit and abilities were not impaired. She had only recently retired from running her own business and still did voluntary work for the Red Cross and made her own clothes.

Alec, fifteen years her junior had been an antiques dealer. Their four-hundred-year-old cottage was like a miniature museum and made Maureen's mouth water.

Up the very steep stairs we went. Alec showed me some of their treasures in the spare bedroom.

On the wall were two pictures of Gladys, ("call me 'Gee', Gladys is so old fashioned", she told me) aged about two or three. One was a charming water colour of her standing on a rustic bridge, the other an enlarged sepia photo taken in 1901 when she was bridesmaid at Aunt Bess's wedding (of "Wiggy Aunt" fame!) How I longed to have those pictures, but one can hardly say to a 97 year old;

"Can I have those when you die?"

She must have realised my covetousness, as next time we visited her a few years later, to my great delight, she gave them to me. They now proudly hang on the wall in our little house. She had no children or other blood relatives so at least they have been kept in the family.

We visited Michael and Jill, Paddy's twin brother and his wife. I was fascinated to see two handsome men in

13

their sixties so completely identical, both as charming and humorous as each other.

During the war when I was thirteen, I went to a boarding school at Stanford Court, a lovely old mansion in Worcestershire. We tried to find it for a sentimental visit, but alas, the gates were closed with KEEP OUT written in large letters. It now belongs to some forestry business, so disappointing.

Still, we went to the old familiar church on the hill and I saw the house and lake in the distance. The memories brought back the distinctive smell of the blacksmith shoeing the horses in the village, when we went there for our weekend walks.

I spent a happy week with Maureen and Paddy, seeing the city, many local beauty spots and attending concerts.

Then came the big treat.

"We're going to Scotland for a few days and you have been invited too."

Paddy drove up the motorway and we briefly stopped at Ullswater in the Lake District to see where the rare golden eagle had nested.

A roster of keen ornithologists watched vigilantly to see no harm came to the nest and optimistically waited for an outcome.

Paddy and Maureen's friends Roger and June welcomed us to their lovely bungalow on the outskirts of Glasgow.

This was my introduction to urban foxes that had become very tame.

Roger fed scraps to them at dusk and we saw them bring the young cubs to feed too, a charming unforgettable sight.

Next day we went sightseeing to Alloway and saw Robert Burns' birthplace, then on to Culzean Castle. We had a guided tour of this impressive 18th century building which overlooks the Firth of Clyde. Sometimes, we were told, you could see across to Ireland.

We went into the city the following day to see the very comprehensive exhibition of Charles Rennie Mackintosh's many talents. I was not aware of the versatility of this 19th century architect and designer. We went for refreshments at the famous Willow tearooms in Sauchiehall Street.

The weather was kind and the following day we appreciated Loch Lomond with the sun shimmering on the waters. Next stop was Arden House in Callender where "Dr Finlay's Casebook", of T.V. fame, had been filmed.

Our return drive to Glasgow was spectacular through long, leafy, winding lanes and sparkling lakes. I managed to control my queasiness.

Roger and Paddy had decided to go mountain climbing the next day, so we three "girls" spent the day in Edinburgh.

I had no idea it was so close to Glasgow. We saw the castle dominating the Royal Mile which stretches to the remains of Holyrood Abbey. It is full of tourist shops, museums and historical landmarks.

It used to have many exclusive shops but they are now more mundane.

Typically, I needed the lavatory urgently and we saw the adjacent Art Gallery so we had a two-fold reason for visiting.

We had individual tastes in art so decided to separate and meet at the Gallery shop in an hour's time.

I happily wandered around admiring the paintings and arrived at the shop a bit early to buy a few cards.

One I saw was a charming painting of a Collie dog and puppies. I felt homesick for my little dog. We had bred Shetland Sheepdogs (Miniature Collies) for years and the litters looked very similar. I thought I'd like to see the original painting but no one knew where it was.

Eventually the Curator was located.

He kindly took me to the basement where shrouded statues loomed over racks and racks of covered, labelled and numbered pictures. He found the original painting which I duly admired. Maureen was amazed that they allowed a member of the public into this sanctum.

After lunch in the crypt at St Giles Cathedral we went to the Toy Museum. There was such a lot to see and many stairs to climb, as different exhibits were on separate floors. What an enchanting place.

A delicious meal at the Highgrove Hotel in Troon completed one of the most exciting, stimulating and enjoyable days I have had.

We returned to Worcestershire the next day as Paddy had a school reunion in Hampshire to attend.

I caught the bus into Worcester and spent a leisurely day looking around this compact ancient city with its Mediaeval and Tudor buildings.

It is famed for its Cathedral where King John of evil repute is buried. I visited the Royal Worcester China complex and also the colourful historic Guildhall.

That evening Maureen and I had a great experience. We visited a local house with spacious lawns to hear a concert.

The night was balmy, the pleasing repertoire was for piano and cello.

The young cellist had recently given birth and we watched fascinated during the evening as she bulged more and more out of her low cut dress. It reminded me of Lady Lowbodice.

> Every time Lady Lowbodice swoons,
> Her boobs pop out like balloons,
> But her butler stands by
> With hauteur in his eye
> And lifts them back in with warm spoons.

Before I said goodbye to them, Paddy gave me a real treat.

I will always miss the history of my birthplace, the culture and the familiarity, but the part of the countryside I have always loved most, is the woods.

Just down their lane is Monkwood, a typical English wood, sheer delight. The three ponds are breeding grounds for both dragonflies and damselflies. Paddy is

17

an odonatologist (lovely word) and escorts groups of enthusiasts to this sanctum.

I just love the sights, smells and ambience of these woods.

On my final evening we visited Michael and Jill. They live about half an hour's drive away.

Goodbyes were said next morning to Maureen and Paddy as Betty collected me to stay with her for a few days in Harrow.

> There was a young lady of Harrow
> Whose views were exceedingly narrow,
> At the end of her paths
> She built two bird baths
> For the different sexes of sparrow.

The temperature was 30°C. and it amazed me how hot I felt. The summer in Perth at the same temperature would just be pleasant as it can occasionally rise to 40°C.

Betty drove us home through the famous, charming and very picturesque Cotswold villages such as Moreton-on-the-Marsh and Chipping Norton. We stopped for lunch at Stow-in-the-Wold. The countryside, enhanced by thatched cottages and old barns, was unbelievably beautiful. We arrived at her home that evening and spent a nostalgic time looking at old photographs.

Peterborough and the Nene Valley railway were our destination the following day. This is the home of the original Thomas the Tank Engine. Catherine, Betty's younger daughter had brought her little boy Ben there to spend the day with us an ideal venue for a four year old.

I had not seen Catherine since she was a curly headed two year old, delightedly chasing Oliver, a similar age, around Kew Gardens to kiss him.

Betty had this event immortalised on an old cine film.

The next day was an unforgettable visit to see Heather, Betty's eldest daughter.

She and her family belong to the Historical Re-enactment Society.

They appear around the country at Fairs and Pageants.

That year they were spending their week's holiday at the Weald and Downland Open Air Museum in Sussex.

This fascinating place on 50 acres has over 50 houses from the thirteenth to the nineteenth century, displayed.

All are original dwellings that have been dismantled and reconstructed. The farms have the animals they would have had at the time and it is a "hands on" experience.

We saw a roof thatcher at work and then we went into a house dated about 1590. Here, Heather was upstairs weaving.

She was dressed as a peasant and had made all their clothes authentically.

Cotton had not yet been discovered, so everything she made was either sewn with wool or flax. Little four year old Alathea, was helping a lady wash the dishes outside, also in the correct attire. This is a genuine old English name. They later had a son called Beric.

Betty had bought a pretty Marks and Spencer dress for Thea, so we all went to their tent for her to try it on. She was wearing no knickers.

Of course, they were not worn in those days. I wondered if Heather was similarly *un*-attired.

The whole Museum was a living authentic restoration of these various periods of English history, a remarkable experience.

Don's niece Valerie's husband Bill, collected me from Harrow and drove me around the Ring Road to their home in Sittingbourne Kent.

Here Valerie had prepared a delicious meal for us followed by what she remembered were my favourites, raspberries and cream.

Later that week, I had the thrill of going raspberry picking with them and could guzzle them to my hearts content. No wonder Kent is called the garden of England. Orchards thrive there and there used to be fields and fields of hops, now mostly gone, but the old oasthouses remain as landmarks of a bygone era.

During the week we went on many visits.

One was to the enchanting Leeds Castle with its beautiful grounds and Culpeper garden. This castle was home to many Queens since it was built in the 12th century. An attraction on the ponds are the black swans. Here in Australia, white swans are a novelty!

Another day we went to Reculver. There we saw the remains of an early Roman fort from the first century. A.D.. and ruins of a very old church.

This Thames-side marshland was where Barnes Wallis secretly tested the bouncing bomb used to bomb the Dams in May 1943.

Rye is a small quaint town that was the haunt of smugglers in the 17th and 18th centuries.

> There was a young lady from Rye
> With a shape like a capital I.
> When they said "It's too bad,"
> She learned how to pad;
> Which shows you that figures can lie.

The tiny lanes and cobbled streets house numerous antique and intriguing gift shops.

We hoped to visit Hastings to bring back memories of when I was seven, but we could find absolutely nowhere to park.

Before leaving them, I admired photos of their younger daughter Clare's wedding and visited Nicola, their elder daughter.

She and Graham had recently bought a captivating house dating from 1750. It had steep stairs and lots of old beams and character, also a lot of renovating work ahead of them.

My holiday was over and Bill drove me to Heathrow after we had said our fond goodbyes.

I boarded the plane for the long and rather tedious flight home, thankful for such a happy and eventful holiday.

CHAPTER THREE

Matzos and mince pies

*Enjoying learning languages, then dabbling in art.
The gourmet group was lots of fun with
knowledge to impart.*

Thursday was a free day for me for some years. I happily attended Trinity School for Seniors, held in Perth. I learned and enjoyed French, History, Tai Chi and Dancing. I attended these and many other classes over the years but I always hoped there might be an option nearer home, one day.

In 1996 I became a founder member of the Armadale branch of University of the Third Age. This international organisation was founded in France in 1973 for the education and stimulation of those of us who have reached the "Third Age" of life.

A very vibrant group initiated this branch and we soon attracted a number of members, both men and women. I served on the committee for a few very invigorating years.

U.3.A. meets twice a month with an interesting speaker and we enjoy an occasional social event. Some members have generously opened their homes to the group for special occasions and parties. Some of the many internal classes I enjoyed were conversational Italian and conversational French. I actually used these when I went overseas in 2000, so I thought I would then try Art. This was a very happy decision as it expanded my mind, my vision and hopefully my abilities.

The first term we had an introduction to drawing, then water colour, then pastels and the final term was acrylic painting. I found that I really enjoyed them all but particularly pastels.

I will never be a great artist but the sense of achievement was enormous when I discovered I could produce a recognisable picture. This was a new creative, satisfying hobby for me.

Coincidentally at this time, I renewed my acquaintance with Doth, the renowned local, very talented and versatile artist. Each Thursday morning whilst her husband used the car, I visited her. She encouraged me in my early attempts at painting. We also indulged in a variety of experimental media such as fascinating solar painting. She is a real inspiration to me as well as becoming a close friend. The sessions degenerated into admiration of Doth's latest creations and the two of us exercising our jaws!

Many other groups existed such as Philosophy, Current Affairs and Music.

One group I joined from its inception was the Gourmet Group. This we limited to twelve people as we visited each other's homes for a meal. The host/hostess provided the food from a certain country or culture,

They then gave a talk and distributed written information to each guest. We had some superb meals in very convivial company.

My first effort was Jewish food. Don offered everyone a pre-prandial drink to mellow them which was just as well. Do I confess? Yes, it is now history. We were to start with "Jewish Penicillin" with matzo balls. (Momma's chicken soup, panacea for everything!) The soup which should be quite clear, went cloudy and the matzo balls disintegrated and had to be fished out and re-moulded. I managed to replace the soup with a very expensive tinned variety! The main course was uneventful but we hoped to enjoy delicious haroset for dessert. These are delectable little flat cakes made from honey, grated apple, almonds and wine. These had also crumbled so I brazenly spooned it into dishes and no-one was any the wiser. What it is to be a "master/mistress?" of bluff!

Meanwhile Don plied them all with wine and a good time was had by all.

I gave a short talk on Kosher food and rituals and gave each guest a Jewish proverb to read out such as

"Even an angel can only do one thing at a time."

Our second effort, cooked by Don and rather ambitious for twelve people, was a traditional Christmas dinner. The research I did on the history and superstitions surrounding Christmas puddings was quite fascinating. They should be made on the twenty-fifth Sunday after Trinity and contain thirteen ingredients (representing

Christ and his disciples.) Everyone in the house had to stir the mixture with a wooden spoon. It had to be stirred from east to west in honour of the three wise men. The Puritans banned the puddings as unfit for God-fearing people but George I, who enjoyed plum puddings, re-established the custom as a traditional part of the Christmas dinner in 1714. I learned lots of interesting and rather useless trivia.

These lunches were held every second month and were thoroughly enjoyed by all of us. We had a variety of menus: Vegetarian, Indian, Vietnamese, Hungarian, Moroccan, Hawaiian and even Australian. We learned how to make gnocchi at the Italian meal.

Eventually the repertoire was exhausted. We all agreed it had been great fun and also educational.

U.3.A. continues to have interesting and varied speakers and I have made many good friends there.

CHAPTER
FOUR

Belly dancers
and tulips

*When Trefoil members meet up, there's a
friendly atmosphere.
Each gathering is held at a different place each year.*

Coincidentally, another group was being formed in
Armadale, the Trefoil Guild. I irreverently call this a
unit for recycled Girl Guides, an apt description. This
group is for anyone who has been involved in Guiding.
I had been on the perimeter as I was enrolled as a
Brownie in 1940 and helped with the embryo Gumnut
Guides in 1990 and both our daughters achieved the
honour of becoming Queen's Guides.

We hold our meeting monthly and once a year have a
"Soup and Slice" day when we invite many other
Guilds to join us for our home cooked lunch and some
enjoyable activities. There is, and always will be, an
incredible sisterly bond between Guides of all ages.

One special pleasure with the Trefoil Guild, is the
Annual State Gathering held at various venues over a
winter weekend — 2001, Albany. 2002, Mandurah.

2003, Kalgoorlie. 2004, Point Walter. 2005, Busselton. 2006, Dale. 2007, Joondalup.

In Albany at the Ace Motel, I was the only one who wanted a single room and had the honeymoon suite complete with a spa, all to myself. What luxury, my first and possibly my last spa. It was very enjoyable but oh dear, it took such a lot of water.

We had a tour of Albany visiting Mount Clarence for delicious tea and scones. Unfortunately the rain that plagued the whole weekend meant we were unable to appreciate the stunning views.

Our AGM was held on the Saturday in the nearby Guide Hall after an interesting talk by the Museum Curator.

On Sunday the bus collected us to take us to Mount Romance with many products relating to Sandalwood and Emu Oil, a sophisticated, commercial enterprise. Then we went to an outlying area to the tiny charming St Werburgh's church built in 1872. There we had an interdenominational service called "Guide's Own". It was difficult to squeeze us all in, but we managed, just.

The Mount Barker Masonic Hall was our venue for a delicious lunch served by the local Guides. The inspiring talk we had about the building informed us that the eighty chairs had all been made from one tree. We visited the Wildflower Factory and had a drive along the picturesque Kalgan River, an enchanting outing in good company.

As at all Trefoil Gatherings, we were given a bag of goodies cleverly decorated by the Guild. Their excellent motto was "Accept progress. Respect tradition".

The following year at Mandurah the theme of the bags was dolphins and we discovered many innovative little gifts as we delved within them. I had rarely visited Mandurah since its rapid expansion some years previously and was surprised at the sophistication and culture of the area. The stylish new Council Chambers was our venue the first evening for some organised games and an opportunity to renew friendships.

The following day one game involved miming each of the Guide Laws. Our little group had "kindness to animals". I was the dog and crawled around lifting my leg against the Advisor's chair, fortunately to her amusement.

We enjoyed a delicious lunch at the Atrium Hotel where we stayed very comfortably all weekend. When the AGM was over we walked to the newly erected, trendy, Performing Arts Centre. On Sunday we visited there again for our annual photo and "Guides Own". We had an enlightening boat trip and saw some huge canal-side mansions. Saturday's evening buffet was enjoyed by all of us and was followed by a talk and a sing-along concluding another pleasurable weekend in good company.

Our train trip to Kalgoorlie, in 2003 took eight dreary hours.

We were happy to settle into our hotel in nearby Boulder that evening but first we had a brief tour of night time Kalgoorlie including the famed red light district of Hay Street. On Saturday our civic reception at the magnificent Town Hall was hosted by the Mayor who had an unpronounceable name. This charming man came and spoke to each of us. After the AGM we were able to tour this amazing, well loved, historical building. The sheer beauty and size of the conference table delighted me.

That afternoon we had a talk about aboriginal languages by a local man. We were all invited to tell of our Guiding experiences. I had little to tell of my own so I told them about Marion's dedication to Guiding. One day she phoned us from Derby where she had been teaching for some years.

"Mum, guess what, the Brownie's float came second in the Boab festival, oh, and I got married this afternoon."

Not even the first part of the news!

My advice to my children has always been:

a.) Get your priorities right, and
b.) Remember your priorities change.

I often have to remind myself to follow my own advice!

That evening was memorable not only for the scrumptious meal at a hotel but also for the performance of the remarkable group of enthusiastic belly dancers, all ages and sizes, a really joyful entertainment. I was so inspired that I later enrolled for a course locally, but alas! I was no longer supple enough to cope adequately.

Early on Sunday morning we all assembled in Hammond Park with its intriguing minicastle. The barbeque breakfast was cooked by the Kalgoorlie Trefoil Guild. Nola, the Deputy Mayor and also a

Trefoil member, sat next to me, a charming unassuming lady. She had organised a moving "Guides Own".

Later we had the opportunity to browse through the street markets in Boulder at our leisure.

A bus tour in the afternoon showed us the mines at Coolgardie, a visit to Warden Finnerty's house and an interesting, rather technical, State Battery tour showing the extraction of gold and its processing. I was completely ignorant about this.

Our evening meal at the Guide centre was followed by a sing-along of familiar Guide songs and a supper before we returned exhausted after a full day to our motel beds.

The long train journey back to Perth was a big improvement on Friday's journey. I had a window seat and enjoyed seeing the dramatic splashes of colour as a profusion of wildflowers transformed the monotonous landscape, a fitting finale to the weekend.

Our location for 2004 was the hostel at Point Walter.

A near sighted chap from Point Walter
Led a glamorous lass to the altar.
A beauty he thought her,
Until soap and water
Made her look like the rock of Gibraltar.

Our hosts were the Melville Trefoil Guild with expert organisation but no tours at all. We remained in the Hostel the whole weekend. The food was good but reminiscent of a school canteen. After Saturday's inevitable AGM a young fireman told us his very inspiring story of being in New York on 9.11.01.

That evening, a man came to tell us some rather indifferent ghost stories. Our "Guides Own" was held outside the next morning with beautiful river views. The Mayor of Melville, a very vivacious lady, spoke to us. Afterwards the local Guides came and played games and sang songs. Goodbyes, lunch and we all went home.

This was a rather disappointing gathering for me. Firstly, because I felt so cold sleeping in the individual brick building and secondly I felt far from well, as it was only a short while after my shoulder accident and I was rather handicapped with my arm still in a sling.

An enthusiastic group of Dale Trefoil Guild members descended on Busselton in 2005 for the Gathering. It never matters what the weather is like, we can always enjoy ourselves. We stayed in a motel conveniently close to St Mary's Hall and the Guide Hall where events took place. Our afternoon was free after the morning AGM and I enjoyed leisurely renewing my acquaintance with the familiar shops and seeing many new ones. Busselton is growing rapidly. I bumped into some people from Armadale. Yes, I had their children at Pre-School about thirty years ago, but they remembered me!

Our inspiring speaker that evening was the wife of the Bishop of Bunbury. Her achievements in her later years were quite amazing.

On Sunday after "Guides Own", our bus trip stopped first at the famous jetty, then a pleasant drive around to see the expansion in the area. We had a sausage sizzle lunch at the Wildlife Park where we saw a few animals in enclosures and wallabies hopping around. We drove through the very upmarket resort of Dunsborough and stopped at May Yates Guide Camp on the way back. It revived many memories for most of the group. Afternoon tea and farewells back at the Hall followed, then Sheila drove a tired but happy group of Dale ladies back to their homes. How lovely to have door to door service!

We had a year to prepare for our Guild, Dale, to host the Gathering in 2006. Some of our eight members worked very hard investigating accommodation, entertainment, catering and all the details involved in preparation for such an event. One of our members made attractive bags for everyone and we filled them with an assortment of goodies. I bought a number of tiny photo frames and my artist friend Doth, generously donated fifty hand painted miniatures. These were cherished by the recipients.

It was late August and our theme rather prematurely, was "Springtime in Armadale".

On Saturday the rain poured all day, literally putting a damper on our plans. The coach drive into the beautiful, hilly, very wet countryside, took us to Serpentine Dam. After a superb morning tea at the café, the tame galahs, kookaburras and parrots delighted our visitors. A local ex-Guide leader gave an interesting talk on Jarrahdale from the haven of the coach. Lunch at Tumbelgum Farm followed before our return to the Guide Hall and the AGM. We remained there and had an excellent catered meal before the local Guides organised an indoor "camp fire" and singing.

During the afternoon I was able to nip home to check on Don. He had not long been discharged from hospital where he had suffered from pharyngeal dysphasia. Fortunately I was able to sleep at home.

Sunday dawned bright and sunny to our relief. A delectable morning tea awaited us at Chalet Healy in Araluen Botanical Park. The head keeper gave us a talk on the origin and cultivation of tulips, their main attraction. They thrive there because it is so much cooler in the hills.

We held our "Guides Own" in the log cabin there. Passing Japanese tourists stared as a large number of ladies burst into "All things bright and beautiful". We had already surprised a group at lunch on Saturday. We were all chattering as usual. Ann wanted silence to say grace. In the Guide movement the leader only has to raise her hand and everyone does likewise, silently. This occurs from Brownie Guides through to Trefoils, a very effective way of disciplining a group.

We left Araluen for a quick look at the Pioneer Village Markets and returned to the Guide Hall for lunch catered for by a local restaurant. We bade our guests farewell and relaxed after a successful and rewarding weekend.

The 2007 Gathering at Joondalup had to be held in Ern Halliday Hostel as other accommodation was all being used. I always insist on a room to myself as I do not like to share, let alone sleep in a dormitory, fusspot that I am. They gave me the leader's room. Everyone else, including the State and National Advisors, slept in the two adjoining dormitories.

The first evening our talk was about the ship, *The Leeuwin*. The following morning a bus took us to a lovely venue overlooking the ocean for the AGM followed by a scrumptious buffet lunch.

The Perth Trefoil Guild funded the project of a patchwork quilt made in Western Australia by various Guilds, all with Australian themes. This was to be sent to England for use in the Australia room at Foxlease in the New Forest where the first World Camp was held in 1924. This stunning work of art (and love) was on display.

Our treat for the afternoon was to have been a visit to the Maze at Bullsbrook but alas, one of the buses broke down. We had afternoon tea there with the biggest scones I have ever eaten but had to return prematurely.

It was back to the hostel, a meal, a brief sing-along and bed for everyone. It was only about eight o'clock. I could not believe people retire at that hour. Off I went. My room was stark in the extreme. There were two bunks on each side of the room and an overhead light, nothing else. No bedside light or even storage, pegs, curtains or chair.

I could not see to read with the bunk overhead and eventually fell asleep. I awoke about 1.00am with my usual urgent bladder call. I groped my way to the door and tried to open it, nothing happened. I tried two or three times and managed to fumble my way to the light switch. I could then see that the door catch had broken.

Desperate by this time, I thumped on the door. I awoke several sleeping ladies in the adjacent dormitories who feared someone was trying to break in. Two bleary-eyed ladies came to the rescue, opening the door from the outside. Without even bothering to thank them, I shot out to the nearby lavatory — just in time! I returned with explanations and apologies but it was a very unnerving experience.

Drizzle greeted us on the final morning but a few of us stoically strolled around the vast grounds before "Guides Own" and a delicious sandwich lunch. We then said goodbye to old and new friends and headed home.

Each Gathering is different but that is one I shall certainly never forget.

CHAPTER
FIVE

Oliver 1998

I froze with apprehension at the policeman's
forceful knock.
The tragic death of Oliver came as a dreadful shock.

One day that is impressed indelibly on my mind is the tenth of February 1998.

It was exactly a week before the anniversary of my brother Jack's tragic death many years previously.

During that afternoon in a burst of rare enthusiasm, I had been cleaning out the kitchen cupboard and knocked over the chip pan. All the oil spilled over the floor, what a mess! It took masses of paper towels, detergent and determination to clean the area. Fortunately the floor was tiled so it was eventually left immaculate. I would need to buy some more oil for Don's chips.

Very soon after this minor catastrophe, the doorbell rang. Don was sitting watching the cricket so I answered it. To my surprise, there were two policemen, "Oh dear," was my first irrelevant thought "they've come to arrest me for spilling the oil!" It must have been a sub-conscious defensive reaction as I sensed by their solemn faces that they had not brought good news.

"Do you have a son Oliver Day?" asked Police Officer Campbell.

When I told him "yes", he asked if we could go into the kitchen and sit down.

"No" I said, as we never sit in the kitchen. "Come into the sitting room."

I was glad I was sitting down, as he told us that Oliver was "deceased" (horrible expression.) from carbon monoxide poisoning. He had taken his own life. They had found him in his car near the isolated cottage where he had been living in northern New South Wales.

It was some years since we had seen him but he had occasionally phoned. The last time he had talked to me for a long time it was about his struggle with depression. I distinctly recalled my final words to him before he rang off. Remember your Mum loves you. Those words have always been a very consoling memory.

The news of his death came as a horrific shock to Don and me. Although I was shocked, I was not surprised, as I had been aware of his battle with the hopelessness that had plagued him for so long. The police left and I sat there like a zombie unable to accept the horror and feeling totally numb. This sense of unreality stayed with me for a couple of days and probably helped me to cope.

Don didn't want me to phone anyone but I did phone Marion and Carrie and cousin Eve. She was totally shocked too, but very supportive. That night I was unable to sleep at all. I just wept into dear Bella's fur. She was our beautiful, faithful, gentle, understanding little Shetland sheepdog.

Sister Ann from church visited me the following day. After an initial prayer, she gave me immense practical support and advice. "You should go over to New South Wales to view his body to be able to grieve properly" she said. I could not possibly have faced that long, complicated journey alone in my distressed state. Anyway, I preferred to remember him as a smiling, handsome young man.

The local New South Wales police were very helpful and recommended a funeral director in Lismore. He too was most co-operative. I arranged for Oliver to be cremated there after the post-mortem. It was a simple ceremony with only a priest in attendance at my request. They thoughtfully audio-taped the short service and sent me a copy. They assured me that I would receive the ashes during the following week. I then had to arrange with the Public Trustee to deal with his few belongings.

Don's reaction to Oliver's death appeared to be total indifference. This made me even more miserable and overwhelmingly heartbroken and alone. A sympathetic visitor asked me discreetly if Oliver was Don's son! I realised that I just had to take all the responsibilities which had me very apprehensive. I suffered from lack of confidence and am easily intimidated. Don has always handled everything from dealing with bills to telling me what to cook.

A few days later, Cousin Eve kindly took me to a beautiful, peaceful rose garden for coffee as a welcome distraction. There had been no notice in the paper but the letters, cards and messages of sympathy came flowing in, even some beautiful flowers from thoughtful friends. I felt overwhelmed by everyone's compassion and amazed how the news of Oliver's sad death had filtered through. I have over ninety cards and letters that I will treasure and keep forever.

Meanwhile, I was both physically and emotionally vulnerable and tried to combat the overpowering weariness I felt. I had a weird sense of unreality and wretchedness. I waited for the ashes to arrive and had arranged a small memorial service to be held with Father Tony at Serpentine Cemetery. Oliver's ashes were to be placed in a niche in the commemorative wall. Leo, who had been very supportive, had kindly engraved the brass plaque as a gift. It simply stated:"

"In loving memory of Oliver Jonathan Day.
Born 1.6.1964. Died 10.2.1998.
Rest in peace."

No ashes arrived. Not only was I stressed but also frustrated. I phoned the funeral director to be told they should have been sent by air but had gone by road and even then, there had been "unforeseen delays". I felt like a contortionist, I was beside myself! I am a worrier at the best of times and that was *not* the best of times. Knowing how I like a bargain, Oliver would have been amused at me getting a bargain cremation. The fee was reduced as an apology.

As a normal five year old boy, Oliver loved to tease. When I told him to hurry up and get ready for school, he would walk deliberately slowly, placing each foot in front of the other in slow motion. This was always known in our family as "doing an Oliver!" "Hurry up" I'd say "You'll be late for your own funeral" and he was!

The planned service had to be delayed but eventually I collected the package from the Postal Depot. Inside were two plastic boxes taped together. I felt numb with grief and despair with this tangible reality. I now wonder how I managed with the stress and the aloneness. I put on a brave face for the service and coped reasonably well. Cousin Eve drove us to the pretty country cemetery in the bush for Oliver's final resting place. A pity he was not there physically. He would have loved the fiasco. I frequently thank God that He blessed me with a sense of humour even at inappropriate moments.

Just the immediate family, Oliver's friend Bob and Leo gathered at the cemetery in the scorching wind. The temperature was 42°C. Father Tony said a few words as there was no eulogy. Sister Ann played a hymn of the 23rd Psalm, "The Lord is my Shepherd". I always associate that particular hymn with Oliver now and cannot remain dry-eyed when I hear it.

Then came the problem, the boxes did not fit into the niche! Western Australia must have different size niches from the Eastern States. Cousin Eve's husband Mac separated them with his pocket knife and one box fitted in, just. That left me holding a box with the remains of half of Oliver.

"What shall I do?" I whispered to Cousin Eve.

She is as facetious as I am and remembering the old TV Quiz show, pretended to clap and chanted sotto voce, Open the box, open the box. Once again Mac's trusty pocket knife came to the rescue. He severed the tape sealing the box, I walked over to the bush and scattered the ashes. "Good-bye Oliver." He always loved the bush so I feel his legs are there forever.

Grandson Simon, aged nine, who had behaved impeccably, was given the responsibility of flying the kite that Oliver had given me as my retirement present.

"Shure, an' it's a symbol of Oliver's spirit going up to heaven." said Sister Ann.

By then, the wind had dropped and it got caught in a tree. Simon had to climb on to Mac's sturdy shoulders to rescue it.

That night, I did not sleep at all as I realised the dreadful truth, Oliver's promising young life ending so tragically at the age of thirty three. I understand now, how fortunate I was that I did not feel anger, I am not an angry person, neither did I feel guilt as many do in similar circumstances. I just felt an intolerable burden of grief. Although time has softened the shock and horror, the grief will always remain. Oliver did what he wanted to. He was terrified he might not make a success of taking his own life.

For months after his death, when the phone rang I would think "that will be Oliver" but in reality I knew it never could be. As a self-appointed very therapeutic task that first week, I gathered photos of him from babyhood on.

It was all we had pertaining to him. I made a collage of thirty three photos, one for each year of his life, and framed it. It is a perpetual reminder of happy days.

Terrible nightmares, not on any specific subject, continued to plague me for months afterwards. I could not stop myself watching the weather forecast on the television for New South Wales each evening. Subconsciously I *knew* he was no longer there. This habit stopped abruptly later in the year when the first book of my memories *Adamant Eve* was published. Maybe, this was because Oliver had particularly hoped I would record my reminiscences.

A few years after Oliver's death, I received a phone call from the Public Trustee.

"Do you know the whereabouts of Oliver's father?" they asked me.

"He is sitting in his chair a few feet away from me." I answered "Why?"

"Well, you were nominated as his next of kin and we didn't know if he still had a father."

They told me he was entitled to half of Oliver's money.

"What money?" I asked.

I had understood that the initial sale of his few possessions had more or less covered his minor debts. But no, the Public Trustee had taken a long time but had found unclaimed superannuation and other monies Oliver was due. Within a few weeks an envelope arrived addressed to both of us. Inside we found a cheque for Donald Day. I felt very disconcerted until I removed it and underneath discovered another one with an identical amount for me.

We were both totally surprised. With this bequest I bought myself an unusual gold chain with tiny flat links. At my request talented Leo engraved a miniscule "OLIVER" on one link, as a very special reminder of an unexpected, posthumous gift.

For many years I have found card making very soothing, so I made and sent "thank you" cards to the many kind people who had supported me and offered their concern and sympathy throughout this very distressing time. I am sure many of them felt "There but for the grace of God, go I".

CHAPTER
SIX

Happy Memories of Oliver

Animals loved Oliver and he loved girls, that's true.
He learned to read a lot of words when he was only two.

As a baby, talking did not interest Oliver. He only uttered monosyllables such as Dad, Mum, Man, (Marion) and Ca (Caroline). One day, when he was about two, he looked out of the window in our home in England and saw a noisy vehicle heading for the local farm. His little eyes lit up.

"Combine 'arvester" he said with delight, to our surprise. He always loved big words and knew their meanings. His questions were original as were his definitions.

"How long is ever?"

"Do spiders suck their thumbs?"

"What colour is heaven?"

"It hasn't got no nothing in it." A descriptive, triple negative of "empty".

Before he was three, I bought the popular book "Teach your baby to read". I felt very sceptical but we played it as a game. He learned about twenty five words effortlessly by identifying large labels I made of nouns such as table, hand, mummy and carpet. We then started on verbs, jump, clap and wave. Suddenly he lost interest, so I wisely forgot it. When he went to school, he was ready to read and learnt easily so that experiment just proved to me that it could be done.

Oliver's love of science started when he was only four. He had been given a magnet set. After taking the iron filings to bed, he wet the bed. We were the only people in the neighbourhood hanging out rust stained sheets.

His invisible companions, at this age, were two ducks. They even came on the plane with us to Australia. We referred to them as "the illegal immigrants" long before that phrase was in common use.

At bedtime, he demanded his "nigh-night" music. "L' Arlessienne" Suite by Bizet. His love of music continued into adulthood when he sang and played bass guitar in a Group and perfected his career as a "mixer". When he attended Primary School, his teachers were concerned that he was not a good mixer!

From an early age he had a sweet voice. He learned the traditional song "Curra burra wirra canna" made popular by Rolf Harris. He and Caroline went for special singing lessons. The teacher wanted to enter them in the local Eisteddfod. Our family is not competitive and the children did not want to enter, so she refused to teach them, end of story.

Another early compulsion was his interest in naming shapes. At about three, he identified squares, circles, triangles and rectangles and the word he loved, parallelograms.

He always liked girls, even in his pre-teenage years and they loved him. Marion was the local Brown Owl and to the delight of the Brownies, he accompanied them on the Perth to Fremantle Walkabout.

He enjoyed his own company and was not keen on sports or "macho" occupations though he was far from effeminate.

As well as being popular with girls, animals loved him. He walked about the house with our little cat "Lulu" draped around his shoulders. The kangaroos at the Wildlife centre were all attracted to him as were the possums in Fitzroy Gardens in Melbourne, an unforgettable memory.

Oliver's originality also extended to his taste in food. When he was small, we had visited Chelmsford Markets and afterwards enjoyed a cup of tea in a little shop. He drank his usual glass of milk. It was almost lunch time and they had started putting bottles of tomato sauce on the tables. When our scones arrived, he insisted on tomato sauce as a garnish. Why not?

Academically, he could have achieved whatever he wished. He was blessed with an exceptionally retentive memory but he never bothered to study. I heard later that the results of his T.E.E. Physics exam were second top in the State but his marks were scaled down as he had not bothered to hand in assignments. We were never ambitious for him. We just wanted him to find a job that he enjoyed. He had so much potential that was never fulfilled.

His sense of humour was very similar to mine and we shared many funny incidents and black humour. We were also both romantics. Often, the two of us stood entranced, watching the fantastic, everchanging sunsets. I will always miss the warmth of his hugs and his unique personality

A sonnet I wrote two weeks after Oliver's death.

He's closer to me than we have been for years
I feel that he is with me now. I know
That as I think of him, I'm close to tears.
I will not hold them back just let them flow.

A curly headed boy with steps so slow
When told to hurry up. "You will be late
For your own funeral." And lo — -
He really was. He'd laugh at such a fate.

We'd often stand together and just gaze
In wonder at the setting of the sun.
I recollect the many happy days
When life was good for him. But now is done.

No need to say goodbye though we're apart.
The essence of his spirit warms my heart.

CHAPTER
SEVEN

Toy giraffes for babies
1998

Plainchant and pamplemousse,
my French friends live near Beaune.
Exciting trip to Belgium. I found the time had flown.

This holiday had been planned before Oliver's tragic death and I decided to go ahead with it, with reservations. In retrospect, it was a very good diversion for me.

I flew to Heathrow and stayed with Stephen, Don's nephew and his partner Alison for a few days. It is only half an hour's drive from their home to the Airport. It is a similar distance to Gatwick, where he deposited me for a flight to Geneva.

This was to be a new and very exciting experience for me.

Gaby and Cécile whom I had met the previous year in New Zealand, had invited me to stay with them in Meursanges in France for a week. They were nearer Geneva than Paris.

When I arrived at the Airport, it was one of life's unforgettable "golden moments", the huge welcoming smile from Cécile.

Gaby drove us through a long tunnel. We saw spectacular mountains, small, pretty villages and different countryside from the English one I knew.

Gaby had recently retired from his farm and they now lived in a fairly new, seven bedroom, very comfortable home in the little village of Meursanges.

The village is so small I could find it on no maps but it is near the historic town of Beaune.

That first evening we watched a beautiful sunset and just relaxed, me with my little dictionary glued to my hand. It stayed there all week.

Gaby and Cécile were extremely kind to me and somehow we managed to converse.

The first day, they took me for a drive and showed me the walled farm that Gaby had managed for Prince Floret de Merodes. We passed his nearby chateau, very old and tranquil, and also many, many vineyards. This is one of the big wine growing areas of France.

I got a big thrill when I saw a sign proclaiming "Office Municipal du 3éme Age." I knew the movement originated in France.

Everywhere we went, I saw roadside signs proclaiming "Caves." I thought it was a bit weird, caves, in this flat agricultural countryside.

Eventually I looked it up and discovered the word means "cellar." and meant there was wine for sale there.

We also saw large marble quarries.

On Sunday they took me as a treat to the Cistercian Abbey of Citeaux. That year they were celebrating their nine hundredth anniversary; mind boggling. This is one place that I did see tourists as we went for a special Mass that these famous monks were singing in Plain Chant. I find the relaxation of the monophonic music so soothing. It was a very special experience.

We drove back through valleys, vineyards and villages. No shops or auberges (inns) open anywhere. They took me to Brancion, a charming mediaeval village on a hill. We visited the Romanesque church and climbed up the semi-ruined castle with the conical towers that I saw everywhere in this area, to see the panoramic view over the Grosne valley.

We could see right across the Burgundy countryside, the rolling hills and small villages and farms. Later we saw the oldest Roman church in France. It was very stark with huge towers. The cemetery was full of graves with marble plaques.

That afternoon we had a relaxing time at home. Gaby had a rest and Cécile and I packed dragées (sugared almonds) for their grandson Nicholas's baptism.

Some were in boxes to be posted to those unable to attend, the rest were counted into bags, so many white and so many blue.

A tradition that fascinated me was that whereas here we might give a baby a teddy bear, in France, they are given toy giraffes.

They had a large family but only one daughter, Hélène, who lived nearby. She had a darling baby boy called Johany, a name which to my surprise was pronounced "Johnny".

50

The food was delicious with one exception, I do not like fatty meat and they obviously did. I found it very hard to choke down.

Their evening meal lasted a couple of hours and was comprised of many courses in a different pattern from that which I was used to, but very interesting.

A glass of wine was enjoyed with each course, except by me. They were appalled that I do not like wine, unbelievable in this, the prime wine growing area of France!

I was content with water, *always* bottled, even to use for teeth cleaning.

The first course was sliced cucumber followed by charcuterie, various cooked and smoked meats, then we had a tossed green salad on its own. After that, oh horrors, a plate of fatty meat. We then had a slab of local cheese, rather bland, and finally dessert. Each course had, as well as the wine, delicious chunks of real French bread and real local butter. The meal was completed by a glass of Gaby's home made delectable cassis, a blackcurrant drink.

Their local town is the picturesque city of Beaune.

The L'Hotel Dieu, a hospital founded in 1442, was only fairly recently used purely for tourism. Gaby said his father had been nursed there.

It is a fascinating, old, well preserved building, its most striking feature the roof with its multi-coloured Flemish tiles. The buildings nestle around the original cobbled courtyard.

Inside there are many treasures, one of which is the altarpiece polptych of a graphic portrayal of The Last Judgement by Rogier Van Der Weyden.

They have an ingenious slow moving platform that one stands on, to enable one to appreciate all the details of this masterpiece.

We also met the Curé of the local Basilica of Notre Dame who was dressed in ordinary clothes to my disappointment. He is a friend of Gaby's.

Here is an interesting fact about the local Primary school in Meursanges, the tiny village where Gaby and Cécile live. The population is so small now that it does not warrant a school to exist. It is the same in the other small villages, as folk tend to move to the towns nowadays. Rather than leaving the schools vacant, they use them all in rotation. Year One might be in village A, Year Two in village B and so on. Buses collect the children and deliver them to the relevant schools.

We visited an old chateau with very neglected gardens, at Sercy; then on to Taizé.

Maybe it was holiday time but this popular ecumenical venue was almost deserted. The enormous church and hall is usually full of young people that it attracts for prayer, meditation and their unique style of music.

Next day I went to the Supermarket with Gaby. Although the town was inland there was a huge display of fish, live crabs, charcuterie, wines and even clothes.

That afternoon I had an unreal experience. We visited the ancient Cistercian Abbey of Fontenay built in the twelfth century.

As we walked through the cloisters, I had a distinct feeling of "dejá vu".

When I was sixteen at Annecy Convent in England, one of the subjects we studied was Monasticism in the Twelfth century and I recalled drawing a detailed plan of this particular Abbey.

I knew where the refectory would be, and the cloisters.

Isn't it amazing that the memory had laid dormant all those years!

I did not know it was famous for having the hydraulic hammer invented there.

The weather was glorious the day we went to Alise Sainte Reine and climbed the hill to admire the really huge statue on its peak. It is of Veringetorix (lovely name!) who was defeated when the Romans conquered Gaul.

It is really dramatic as it can be seen for miles around because of its position and size.

Later when we visited the very beautiful Chateau of Bussy-Rabutin, I was surprised at the portraits with satirical cartoons and quotations. Apparently the flamboyant Roger de Bussy-Rabutin was a famous libertine of the 17th century.

Up the steep hill we climbed to Flavigny-sur-Ozanain. This very well preserved village was where the film "Chocolat" was made.

On our return I had a delicious glass of "pamplemousse" to drink. I did remember that delightful translation of the word "grapefruit."

On my penultimate day, we had a rather long drive to visit the city of Dijon. I bought Don a pot of their famous mustard there.

This was another place where we did see a lot of tourists.

It is a wonderfully preserved old city, bursting at the seams with churches, cathedrals and museums. There is even a museum dedicated to mustard! We visited a few until I was satiated. The charming little lanes had very ancient half-timbered houses, still inhabited, even though some dated from the 15th century.

We saw the Palace of the Dukes of Burgundy and the very well preserved and presented Musée d'Arts.

We went to a square that had some exquisite statues, dating from the 18th century, mainly of naked men. It is known as "Rude Square" not because of these statues but because the sculptor's name was François Rude!

On my final day it happened to be Ascension Day, so we went to Mass at a lovely old church in a nearby village. The local country women really looked as I would have imagined, with their long skirts and headscarves.

The lengthy drive to Geneva airport along the Autoroute, was broken briefly for a bladder stop. Gaby sat in the car and within seconds was sound asleep. I was fascinated with the immediacy of his relaxation. Cécile explained that he just needed ten minutes, then would be fit to resume the journey.

We said "au revoir" fondly, before I left on the short flight back to England.

It was a wonderful, very different, exciting adventure for me with such a kind and charismatic couple.

My French certainly improved, even in that short time.

Stephen met me and the following day drove me to Fittleworth for another weekend course.

This time it was entitled "Write your Autobiography." For a long time I had toyed with doing this.

The class of fourteen was too big, as we all had to read what we had written to the group at each session, and that took a long time. My efforts were abysmal compared with many of the others, some of whom were professional writers.

He started by asking us why we were doing the course.

I wrote that I hoped to learn from others, to become inspired and to get the impetus to actually write.

At the end of the course John, the tutor, asked us to write how we had felt now it was completed. I wrote that I felt totally inadequate, inhibited and disheartened.

Something must have affected me though, as the following year I actually published the first volume of my memories.

Stephen collected me from Sussex and we returned to his home where I briefly met Robert and John, his handsome young sons, before a visit to beautiful Painshill Gardens.

It amazed me that driving along the roads in Surrey, nothing seemed to have changed from forty years ago when I had lived there. The countryside was unspoiled, the landmarks unchanged, wild strawberries still grew in Rectory Lane.

Stephen reminded me of the "Green Belt" policy to half development in rural areas and prevent the urban sprawl.

He drove me to Essex where I spent a few days with Douglas and Margaret, our friends and neighbours, and visited some old friends. They also took me sightseeing.

Then I went to nearby Brentwood to catch up with my dear friend Nickey and family.

Adam their son is very dutiful in always visiting Eve when I am there, how apt!

I also saw their daughter and my goddaughter, Elaine who lives in Tollesbury. I was able to meet her young family.

Bill drove up from Sittingbourne in Kent to collect me to spend a few days with them.

One windy, wet day we went to Margate, now rather sleazy, and visited Westgate briefly. The hotels on the Front were almost the same as I remembered from a small child. The photo on the cover of *Adamant Eve* was taken there in 1934, rather a long time ago. Everything seemed so much smaller and scruffier.

We went to Broadstairs and saw Dickens' home at Bleak House. The weather was definitely bleak that day too.

On our return we passed St Augustine's Cross at Ebbsfleet. This commemorates the bringing of Christianity to England in 597 A.D..

We saw an unbelievably blue field of linseed, what a magical sight.

Bill took me back to Twickenham and Jack's home for a day or two.

I had a free day and had the opportunity to spend it with my new friend Barbara.

56

I had met her in Australia briefly, a year or so previously when she came to one of our "Thinking Day" celebrations with the Trefoil Guild, whilst she was on holiday in Armadale.

We stayed in touch and she kindly collected me and welcomed me to her lovely home. She had invited some of her Trefoil friends for lunch to meet me too, a very happy experience.

Dear friend Betty from Harrow, collected me and we had a few days together in her home where we had intimate chats and happy reminiscences.

Faithful nephew Stephen (he always called me his favourite aunt!) drove up from Surrey and valiantly took me across the country to Worcestershire and Maureen and Paddy.

We had a few days relaxing and visiting some lovely locations.

One day we went to very hilly Malvern and visited the Abbey. I found that it had an exceptionally spiritual atmosphere.

Afterwards we had lunch in their little café.

I had one of the most delicious soups I have ever tasted. It was broccoli and almond.

When I asked to congratulate the voluntary cook, to my surprise it turned out to be an elderly man.

Another day we went to Birmingham.

We visited the Barber Institute of Fine Arts where Maureen was a voluntary Guide, then a tour of the city. There were a lot of huge new buildings alongside old and historical ones.

The following day I had a huge treat in store, we were to visit Belgium.

We had a long drive to Dover and boarded the ferry with the car.

It took seventy five minutes to cross to Calais and, thank God, the sea was calm. I had nervously dosed myself with tablets, as I am a notoriously bad sailor.

There was a young cashier of Calais
Whose accounts when reviewed wouldn't talais.
But his chief smelled a rat
When he furnished a flat
And was seen every night at the balais.

Here I was in France again.

This time we drove through Dunkirk to Ypres in Belgium. This very old city had been rebuilt after its devastation during World War I.

The Menin Gate Memorial commemorates over 55,000 Commonwealth soldiers who died during the war and have no known grave. I found it very moving.

We had quite a long drive through the countryside of Belgium until we reached Knokke on the coast.

This seaside town is where many influential people have their holiday homes.

These exclusive mansions are maintained by a minimal staff, except for the one month of the year when they are used.

Long time friends of Maureen and Paddy owned a lovely Colonial style home right in the centre of town. One emerged from the driveway, right into the market place.

This house was built on two and a half acres of landscaped gardens. The well kept flower beds and rolling lawns were enhanced by a number of magnificent mature trees.

The house was built in the 1920's and has retained the atmosphere of the period. Most of the rooms have the original furnishings, really amazing.

There were ten bedrooms and large living areas.

There was a huge bath in the middle of a vast bathroom but it takes such a lot of water, it was rarely used.

Each bedroom had its own handbasin.

When we arrived we were pretty tired after the long journey.

We were greeted graciously and a meal awaited us before our hosts departed. Sebastien their adult son thoughtfully had the Australian flag flying to greet me.

The next morning we ventured into the adjacent bustling colourful markets.

Men and women were both buying flowers and the many fruit, cheeses and other stalls seemed to be doing brisk business.

"Let's go out for a coffee" Paddy suggested.

A mere ten minutes drive and we were in Sluis in Holland. I could hardly believe we were in another country with no formalities and so very close.

This old historic town was severely damaged during the war, but most of the buildings have been restored including the typical windmill actually rotating — just what I expected to see in Holland.

The people here, as in Knokke, speak Flemish.

It was a pretty town by the canal and very busy too.

The shops all shut from midday until one thirty for lunch.

That afternoon the charming family who owned the house visited us. They drove us around the huge mansions and past the "M'asTu Vu"? (have you seen me?) Square where the young folk promenade to show off to each other!

We had a walk on the pleasant sandy beach and paddled.

I was told to help myself to the delicious, tiny, wild strawberries that grew behind the house. These were a real treat, quite unlike the cultivated variety, much sweeter with a delicate taste.

The next day we drove to Bruges. This is a very busy town, popular with the local people as well as the tourists.

Two of the huge churches were closed, a pity.

We ventured into the rather dark and very ornate Basilica of the Holy Blood.

This phial was brought to the city by the Crusaders and each year there is a procession of over a thousand people in its honour, some dressed as knights and Crusaders.

The architecture of the Provincial Hall and City Hall were awe inspiring in their ornamentation.

We saw the huge eighty three feet high Belfry tower.

It has 366 steps up a steep narrow stairway to reach the top, not for me, thank you.

The Béguinage was a large walled area enclosing houses originally for poor and elderly women. There had always been a surplus of such women as so many of their menfolk died in battles, down the ages.

We had our lunch of baguettes in a shady square where to my surprise a group of English Morris Dancers were giving a demonstration.

Maureen and I went for a boat trip on the canal and saw a different aspect of the houses and businesses in this thriving city.

One thing Bruges is famous for, is its lace.

There are little lace shops in most of the side streets.

On our way home to Calais we stopped at the town of Damme and admired their beautiful 14th century Town Hall. It was a picturesque town. We had a walk by the peaceful river.

We then drove across to France and Paddy actually drove the car on to the large ferry. Then we walked on the deck and I was delighted that I did not feel queasy, though I had taken my tablets as a precaution.

The formalities at Dover, although tedious and slow, were uneventful.

Then Paddy faced the long drive across England back to Worcestershire and home. Whew! That was a lot of travelling in one day.

That evening I took Maureen and Paddy out to a well deserved meal at a pretty pub in a nearby village.

I had a day on my own in Worcester, as I love to explore this very old interesting city.

Once again I visited the Royal Worcester complex and saw a very fascinating film about the products. I visited their museum and saw some awe-inspiring items. Everything there was very, very expensive.

That evening we went to Birmingham Oratory where we heard the unaccompanied Ex Cathedra choir sing Rachmaninov's Vespers.

We spent a morning at Wyre Piddle seeing a rather shrunken but still lively cousin "Gee" and Alec. I discovered that she was born in 1899 so would be a hundred next year. She was quite amazing.

Next day we went to Ludlow. This Shropshire city is on the Welsh border.

The large castle dominates the area. We also saw the beautiful, half timbered Feathers Hotel and other similar architecture.

What amazed me, was the clothing store Bodenhams, that had been trading for six hundred years.

It was Festival Week and all sorts of exciting activities were taking place.

Male students, dressed up as female nurses, were racing hospital beds with outrageously dressed "patients" up the steep streets.

It was a great day to visit the city.

Maureen's brother Noel, who I remembered as a teenager, and his wife Biddy live at Cranleigh in Surrey.

We all drove down there and had a happy day or two with them in their lovely home, before Maureen and

Paddy drove me the relatively short distance to Heathrow.

Fond farewells said, I faced the long, tedious journey home, but what an eventful, exciting, unforgettable holiday I had experienced.

CHAPTER EIGHT

Encounter with the "devil" 1999

Apple growing, chocolate making mysteries unveiled.
Beautiful Port Arthur where criminals were jailed.

One of my ambitions had always been to visit Tasmania.

In autumn 1999, this was finally achieved. I booked a tour of the island with an excellent coach company.

I arrived in Launceston after an uneventful short flight from Melbourne.

Our first stop was at Grindelwald, a reproduction Swiss Village. This was brainchild of Roelf Vos who sold his supermarket chain to Woolworths about twenty years previously.

This quaint town had shops of Swiss memorabilia and foodstuffs and was a popular tourist attraction.

Tastes at one of the many boutique wineries followed. I did not mind being a non-wine drinker as there was a good selection of cheeses and biscuits.

I chatted to a charming Welshman who was also travelling alone on the tour. After that, he pointedly avoided me. Did he think I was chasing him?

Our early start the next day took us to Cataract Gorge. This is not far from Launceston. I enjoyed the ride in the chair lift and gasped at the natural beauty of the area.

We visited a beautifully furnished old home. I was surprised that they trusted unsupervised visitors with all the lovely old articles on display. I hope they did not lose any.

I sat in an old school desk at the Derby tin mine complex. The shanty town had many interesting old buildings,

That night at the Hotel, my room overlooked Salamander Beach, a real joy.

As I am an animal lover, Bicheno Wildlife Park delighted me. It is a huge area and rehabilitates many endangered species. The one I found most fascinating was the Tasmanian Devil. This vicious marsupial is as big as a large dog. The keeper had one he showed us called Minnie, it smelt horrible. It is said it can have a worse odour than a skunk. In relation to its body size, it has the strongest bite of any mammal. It only has one set of teeth that grow slowly all its life but what incredibly vicious ones they are. They can easily crunch up a small animal including all the bones. I plucked up courage to tentatively stroke her bristly coat.

Later on I had the undiluted pleasure of holding a young wombat, I had not realised their size.

The drive to Freycinet Lodge, our next resting place, was through spectacular countryside. The weather had become very blustery and the rain pounded against the roof of the individual chalet where I slept that night.

65

The usually azure sea was dull the next morning, as grey as the ominous granite mountains that we drove by. We were assured that the scenery is magnificent and told to return when the weather was kinder. We heard later that it was the worst storm they had experienced for twenty four years. Just our luck!

Later the sun came out as we headed across the "Spiky Bridge" to Port Arthur.

The scenery became more spectacular the nearer we got to our destination.

I think the majestic scenery around Port Arthur is amongst the most outstanding I have ever seen. Many on the tour found the sadness and tragedy of the place prevented them from wallowing in the sheer wonder of this incredible area.

The Penal Settlement was started in 1830 for the worst criminals and those who had re-offended. In 1855 they built the "new" prison with 80 individual cells and instead of the brutal whippings the convicts had been subjected to, they were given the "silent treatment", each having to wear a hood when out of his cell, such as the compulsory weekly attendance at church.

The place had natural security with shark infested waters on three sides and prison officers and guard dogs on the isthmus of the fourth.

The prison was closed in 1877 and in 1895 a devastating fire destroyed most of the buildings, leaving the ruins we see today. This is when the small town was established.

We had a boat tour around Dead Island where many of the prisoners were buried.

In 1996, Port Arthur was the scene of the horrific mass murder by Martin Bryant of 35 people, another 37 were wounded. Three years later the memories were still all too vivid for the residents.

The following day we had Tasman's Arch, Devil's Kitchen and an uninspiring blow hole pointed out to us on our way to charming Richmond. Here we had an opportunity to wander and I discovered an exciting bookshop set up in an ordinary house, irresistible.

After lunch we reached Hobart and visited the Botanic Gardens and Mount Wilson. We had a short cruise on the beautiful calm waters of the Derwent River.

The next day we took the ferry at Kettering for the twenty minute ride to Bruny Island. I would have liked to have seen more at Bligh Museum but time was limited.

At Huon we were all given an apple to eat while we watched the apple processing plant, very impressive.

I often enjoy smoked salmon that comes from Tasmania, at Huon we also saw a video about the local salmon farming.

Yum yum! Cadbury's chocolate factory was our destination the following day.

The various tastes of Cadbury's Dairy Milk chocolate fascinate me. I have enjoyed it in England, New Zealand and Australia in the identical blue wrapper, and they all taste different.

I think the creamiest comes from New Zealand. Maybe their high rainfall makes the grass the cows graze on really lush.

When our group entered the factory we were given a talk on the history of Cadburys and how chocolate is made. We had been warned not to have open toed shoes and were now given hair nets and ear muffs to wear. Their standards are necessarily strict. The machinery was very noisy.

We saw various procedures, mostly automated and after each section were given some chocolates to taste. The wrapped ones I pocketed for later.

When she was small, Marion loved to get a bar of "Five Boys" chocolate.

I could never remember all the descriptions of the boys' expressions. Here an old advertisement reminded me, they were: Desperation, Pacification, Expectation, Acclamation and Realisation.

I found the tour not only delicious, with all the tastes they gave us but also very educational. I was particularly interested, as at the time I enjoyed making chocolates as gifts. I melted it, put it in moulds and added various fillings, such as fondant, nuts or fudge and then sealed them with more chocolate. At Christmas time, as I enjoyed fiddling, I would colour white chocolate painstakingly using a toothpick with various powder colours. Anything liquid "kills" the gloss. I might have made a rose with a pink flower and green leaves or Father Christmas with red hat and a white beard.

It was extremely time consuming, seeing that they took one minute to be gobbled up, but they were fun to make.

I have always loved coffee flavoured sweets and wanted some special oil that can flavour the actual chocolate. I already had orange oil.

I finally found some in England in Harrods. I bought it. Soon after, I had to visit their "Ladies Room". I could smell this strong coffee aroma permeating the room. The top of the little bottle had not been secure and it had leaked over everything in my handbag. I returned to the department to complain in my most aristocratic voice.

"So sorry Madam, of course we will replace it."

I examined the bottle later and discovered the label said "Made in Australia!"

I had arranged to meet my friend Anne's daughter at the hotel.

She and her husband had recently moved to Hobart.

I had not seen Jennifer since she was a little girl. She used to have straight dark hair with a fringe, a chubby face and a lovely smile.

Would I recognise her?

I had no problem, I saw the same hair style, but no chubbiness now, as the slim, graceful, young lady came towards me with a warm, recognisable, sweet smile.

We spent a lovely afternoon together. She showed me some of the historical areas of the city.

After lunch she indulged me in my latest passion, by taking me to see the manufacturers of rubber stamps that I use for making cards. We found the small private house eventually and the helpful welcoming couple that ran the business.

This was a very pleasant diversion from the tour.

We were unable to see Mount Wellington as it was misty throughout our brief stay.

On our way to Strahan, we stopped at Russell Falls. Here were the tallest trees I had ever seen. I think they were Swamp gums. Tall tree ferns lined the pathway.

We stopped briefly at Queenstown. The stark "moonscape" scenery is due to the deposits in the rock with a pinkish hue. Copper mining had ceased and the town seemed to be rather a drear and desolate place, made more so by the constant drizzle.

The next day we headed for Strahan and went for an intriguing cruise up the Gordon River. This was an exciting visit to a rainforest and aptly it was raining.

Everything was very green and luxuriant.

We saw trees that were over 2000 years old and Huon pines and Myrtle trees. Because of the high humidity, everything was covered in bright green lichen.

We passed some beautiful waterfalls and pools. Everything, including us, seemed to be decidedly damp but I found this a very inspiring experience.

After lunch we visited the Mining Museum at Zeehan, I felt satiated with information.

We had a special champagne dinner that evening as it was the final one of the tour.

On our last day we drove along the rugged country of the north coast. First we saw forests, then agricultural land and finally the orchards for which Tasmania is famous.

The tractor-drawn "Granny Smith Express" awaited us at AVRO orchard to give us a tour. We then sat on crates munching apples to watch a very good film.

One ninety year old apple tree had 277 varieties grafted on to it.

We had a demonstration of the original apple peeler that was used and then saw the automated one. The grading of the fruit was very strict particularly for the export market.

We then headed for the airport, our trip was finished.

This visit was an apt finale to an educational and interesting tour.

I felt I was in a different country and could not believe that when I sent a postcard, it cost the same as if it was sent locally.

I was reminded of the size and diversity of this great country.

CHAPTER
NINE

Wet knickers in Paris 2000

Tour around beautiful Ireland, a very wet trip
on the D.A.R.T.
In Italy, France, we all marvelled at buildings and
sculptures and art.

Pope Paul II declared the year 2000 as a year of Pilgrimage. Our Parish at St Francis Xavier's Armadale decided to have a really adventurous one. We were supported and encouraged by Father Tony our Parish Priest and Sister Ann, our Parish Assistant who both hoped to be able to join us.

Planning started a few years prior to the event. Firstly, we needed to know *who* was interested, then *where* we would go and then of course the *cost*.

Margaret worked really hard finding out various options and prices and bringing them to meetings where we sifted them through and made decisions. We planned an exciting itinerary and with a little effort we had twenty six enthusiastic, optimistic pilgrims.

(One of Father's criteria was that we would not start too early in the morning.)

Personally, it was an ideal opportunity for me to achieve my ambition to also see Ireland. The few days we would be there on the Pilgrimage would not have sufficed. So I booked an independent Trafalgar Tour immediately prior to the arrival of the other pilgrims in Dublin, with just one extra free day there. I decided to leave two weeks earlier than the others and spend a week with dear Maureen and Paddy in Worcester and then fly to Dublin from Birmingham.

September arrived at last. Plans completed, farewells said and Gillian kindly drove me to the Airport. The only flight available then, was a very long one, via Johannesburg where we had a pleasant enough three and a half hour's break. I enjoyed wandering around the airport on my one and only visit to Africa! I noticed that security was extremely strict.

As often happens on a flight, I could feel myself developing a cold. There are so many people and germs in a confined space. As we descended to Heathrow I had a brief but terrifying awareness of being totally deaf.

I was met by Paddy and Maureen and half the following week they spent tenderly nurturing me back to health. Their local chemist made his own cough mixture, a linctus, with a base of creosote, delicious. It was known as "Mr Ogle's jolop".

Alas, chemists no longer make their own medicines.

On Wednesday, Maureen took me to visit my ancient cousin "Gee". She survived in good health with all her faculties until she was 103. Alec her husband looked very dapper wearing a bow tie that she had made to match her outfit. She was still making her own clothes.

We had received a postcard in Australia telling us that the B.B.C. were broadcasting a programme the following day called "100 Years Young."

This fascinating documentary interviewed a number of centenarians. They questioned her with her sewing group. Fortunately, I was able to phone my nephew and he recorded it for me. It is something I will always treasure for its inspiration.

One day we visited Birmingham for their Artfest. After seeing the very impressive Town Hall, we wandered through the throngs of people enjoying the many activities. We listened to a Steel Band, watched a mock wedding and craft displays. We also appreciated the various talents of the many buskers. I had my photo taken with two outrageously dressed men, just for fun.

The weather was kind and it was good to see so many people just having a good time.

Paddy drove me to the airport very early for my flight to Dublin. First we settled into our comfortable hotel room before being taken on a comprehensive tour of the city. At dinner that evening we got to know some of our fellow tourists. Everyone but me seemed to have an Irish surname and were undoubtedly visiting Ireland to see the land of their ancestry. They hailed from U.S.A, Canada, South Africa and many parts of Australia.

Our coach tour started the following day heading south to Waterford. We visited the National Stud Farm where the magnificent animals were bred and cherished. They warned us that the studs can be very vicious.

We had a couple of hours free in Kilkenny. All I could think of was the old rhyme:

There once were two cats of Kilkenny,
Each thought there was one cat too many,
So they fought and they fit
They scratched and they bit
'Til excepting their nails and the tips of their tails,
Instead of two cats there weren't any.

As I walked through the streets I had to pinch myself and say, "Yes, I really am in Ireland at last."

I was lucky enough to be in the famous Black Abbey, built in the 13th century when Mass was being celebrated, this was an unexpected bonus. It is said to be called the Black Abbey because of the black capes the Dominican Fathers wear.

The very stylish showrooms at Waterford Crystal were amazing. The atmosphere of sanctity was such that I almost felt we should speak in whispers. All the crystal articles were creatively displayed, incredibly expensive but a joy to behold. We even saw a grandfather clock completely made of crystal, awe inspiring.

The following day we drove through some very attractive countryside to Blarney Castle, a very, very tall structure. I know my limitations, and did not attempt to climb the 105 steps. I happily watched the others labouring up there to kiss the famous Blarney Stone.

I walked around the gardens and was surprised, delighted and literally relieved to see a sign saying "Lavatories". (not, Toilets or Ladies and Gents). They obviously, like me, call them lavatories in Ireland.

It was a bright sunny day as we drove around the "Ring of Kerry". The scenery with the sparkling lakes, sandy beaches and mountains rising above them was just glorious. This was the Ireland I had always imagined, unspoiled and oh, so green.

I think what surprised me most, was the prosperity everywhere. I had always imagined simplicity and lack of sophistication, how wrong I was.

Killarney with its beautiful lakes brought back the old song Dan Maloney sang:

> "By Killarney's lakes and fells,
> Emerald isles and winding bays,
> Mountain paths and woodland dells,
> Memory ever fondly strays."

We had a short while in Limerick to buy our lunch. I could not waste time in this busy city on such a mundane thing. Actually being *in* Limerick, I had to find a bookshop and I bought a couple of limerick books there.

We visited the enormous Church of Ireland, St Mary's Cathedral before we left.

Craggannowen, a replica mediaeval village was our next stop. We saw how the Celts arrived and saw their tribal dwellings. Costumed guides showed us around the Iron Age and Early Christian homes. It was a living museum and very interesting but our visit was all too short.

I went to Sunday Mass in a lovely Franciscan church in Galway, I had my money ready and was very surprised that there was no collection.

We stopped briefly at Athlone on the way to Dublin, all was very quiet there as it was Sunday.

We settled into our Dublin hotel then were taken to 29 Merrion Square to visit a Regency house beautifully and authentically furnished. That was the final day of the tour so we said our "goodbyes" and people were taken to their respective Airlines.

I always knew I would love Ireland and I was not disappointed. I loved the beautiful countryside and the historical cities but most of all, I loved the warmth of the people.

The last few days I had become friendly with a pleasant couple from Canada, Rob and Sue also Peter from Melbourne who was travelling alone and spending a further week in Dublin. He and I decided to spend the following day together as I had just one day before meeting up with the Armadale pilgrims.

We decided to explore Dublin by travelling on the "Dart", (Dublin Area Rapid Transit) the suburban railway that runs north and south along the coast. We each bought an all-day pass.

First we went south to Bray, with lovely sea views all the way. We had lunch and explored a while. It started raining so we were glad to return to the train and then alighted at the busy port of Dun Laoghaire and watched the large ferry arrive from Wales. People were milling around collecting luggage, re-uniting with friends and there was almost a carnival atmosphere. When we caught the next train it coincided with the end of the school day and was packed with students in various uniforms and behaving as students do!

We stayed on until we reached the northernmost point, Howth. The rain had turned to a light drizzle and we stopped there for a welcome afternoon pot of tea. The views of Dublin Bay were clear in spite of the weather.

We eventually returned to our respective hotels and said goodbye after a very pleasant day in good company. I have stayed in touch with Peter via email, as I have with Rob and Sue, too.

The following day I went to Dublin Airport with my luggage to meet the Armadale pilgrims who had just arrived after the long flight from Perth. They all looked exhausted. It was good to see the familiar faces as we boarded the coach for the rather perilous drive across the country to Knock in County Mayo.

This town was home to Sister Ann and her sister Bridie who joined us there for the rest of the Pilgrimage. The food and accommodation were excellent and I was pleasantly surprised with the spiritual ambience of the Shrine that was adjacent to our hotel. It was in 1879 that fifteen people saw an apparition of Mary, St Joseph and St John. Over a million and a half people now visit this Marian Shrine annually but it has not become too commercialised.

We all slept well that night and were ready the next day to explore the large, well laid out complex, various chapels, the Basilica and the Chapel of the Apparition where Father Tony said Mass.

There seemed to be flowers everywhere, both inside the chapels and in the colourful gardens. In the afternoon we walked the Stations of the Cross around the grounds, a very moving experience.

When it was time to leave, true to tradition, it rained all the way from Knock to Dublin. We stopped for coffee and cakes at Mullingar and had another stop in the drizzle when a few brave folk walked up the sodden hill to photograph some 5,000 years old burial mounds.

Once we arrived in Dublin we went to our place of residence which was actually in the student's quarters of the famous Trinity College in the heart of the city. That afternoon I braved the crowds and queued to admire the remarkably preserved Book of Kells. This magnificent volume was produced around 800 A.D.. and contains the four gospels in Latin, with beautifully illuminated calligraphy and ornamental pictorial knotwork.

I marvelled at the Library in the Long Room. There are said to be over two hundred thousand antiquarian books and altogether more than six million books, mind boggling.

The following day was free. Most of us attended Mass at an ornate Carmelite church not far away. It was the speediest Mass I have ever heard, less than twenty minutes!

I decided to go to the Information Centre to see what options I had and decide how I would spend the day. I met a man there, Paul, on a similar mission. He told me he had come to Dublin from England to see the play *Mutabilitee* as a friend of his was involved.

We stopped on our city exploration tour for a coffee and he told me he was an author.

This day happened to be Dublin's first ever car-free day and all the buses were free. Paul had a luncheon date so I happily sat and watched an outdoor rehearsal of a very high quality T.V. production of Bizet's Carmen, a favourite of mine. I always feel it is the unexpected event such as this, that makes a holiday exciting.

I then happily wandered around the back streets.

Two shops in particular enchanted me. One was a very well stocked second-hand bookshop with books spilling out of their shelves and stacked in the street. The other was a real old fashioned, traditional sweet shop. Tall jars of colourful favourites such as humbugs, sherbet lemons and fruit drops decorated the window and interior of this friendly shop. The elderly proprietor was delighted when I asked if I could photograph this gem.

I visited St Patrick's Cathedral and another really ancient ornate church that was full of people mumbling prayers and lighting candles.

I was intrigued by the beautiful building of the National Museum of History and Archaeology. I went inside briefly and marvelled at the impressive cupola in the foyer as one enters. I would have loved to have had unlimited time to explore this museum. During our previous week's tour our excellent Guide had given us a taste of the diversity of Irish history and I was eager to know more.

I then had a quick look at a large shopping centre and visited the famous Clery's Department Store before returning to the college for our meal.

Kath and I thought we would find the College Theatre where *Mutablitee* was showing. Father Tony and his brother Terry joined us for this dark, weird play, set in the seventeenth century. It involved Shakespeare, Edmund Spencer and an Irish King and I found it totally confusing. The modern backdrops bewildered me even more, nonetheless, it was an experience.

It seemed as if it took us the whole of a tedious day to fly from Dublin to Rome via Gatwick with various delays. Still, here we were, at last in Rome.

On our first day in the "Eternal City" we wended our way by Metro to St Peter's Square. There had been about 500,000 people there as the Pope had just left after saying Mass.

Later that week an elderly Cardinal had died and we were actually lucky enough to glimpse "El Papa" (the pope) as he said the Requiem Mass. I find St Peter's spellbinding and humbling. I actually had one of the two spiritual moments of the tour there. I forged my way through the milling crowds to enter the Chapel of the Blessed Sacrament which is reserved for private prayer. The spiritual ambience was almost tangible.

It is such a moving experience to see the original "La Pieta."

After lunch of a very indifferent pizza near the Vatican some of us went on the "hop on hop off" bus.

I spent quite a while at the impressive Colosseum amazed at its age and the skill of the men who had built this huge structure so long ago.

A few men were dressed as centurions especially for photographers.

It is obviously a popular place for wedding photos. It was Sunday and we saw three separate brides and grooms there.

When the tour was originally being planned, I said that on my free day I intended visiting Pompeii, a long held ambition of mine.

"I'm coming too," said Kath.

"Me too." said someone else.

In the end, it became the first part of our actual coach tour. The drive there was long but very interesting. After lunch we had a two hour guided tour of the extensive ruins of the town that had been smothered in ash when nearby Mount Vesuvius erupted in 79 A.D.. I was surprised at the quality of the preserved buildings and realised what a sophisticated lifestyle they had as we saw baths, brothels and bakeries. There was such a lot to observe and absorb, I felt bewildered and satiated. It was a wonderful experience and worth waiting a lifetime for.

The Sistine Chapel was crowded as always, when we visited and had recently been restored. It is a cornucopia of colour and visual indulgence, a tribute to Michelangelo's genius. The Vatican Museum was well laid out with Roman and Greek statues and Etruscan Art. There was so much to see and we only saw a fraction of it.

As we went for some much needed refreshment in the Museum Café, Father Tony was greeted by some West Australian folk he had recently been involved with. It is a small world!

After our meal that evening Bruno our driver took us for a night time tour. We stopped at the Trevi Fountain where some threw in coins. This means one will return some day. We went for a stroll to soak up the magic atmosphere of this fabulous city.

The next day we met our guide Laura. She gave us an excellent commentary as we headed north into Umbria. Perugia is perched high on a steep hill involving escalators to my surprise, as well as endless steps. When one reaches the summit, this ancient city has unparalleled views.

I rarely stopped during our lunch breaks as I did not want to waste precious time and opportunity. I tended to eat "on the run". I visited the Galleria (Art Gallery). This was free to European pensioners. I was ridiculously thrilled to be able to show my U.K. pension card!

In the foyer I saw the most enchanting small bronze statue of a 15th century warrior on his horse. It was just exquisite and I stood and gazed entranced. It was one of life's golden, unforgettable moments. My delight was surprising, as I am not a "horsey" person and definitely not into warriors.

At last my life's ambition was to be achieved. We were to visit Assisi, the home of my favourite saint, St Francis.

Oliver chose the name Francis as his confirmation name. When the bishop interviewed him and asked him why he had chosen this particular saint, he was expecting a reply that Oliver loved animals as St Francis did, or that he admired his humble philosophy, but no, Oliver replied the reason he chose that name was that "his mother would kill him if he didn't!"

Alas, more escalators and more steps and even more. By the time we arrived there after the Perugian adventure, I was totally exhausted. To quote Father Tony, "We were almost dead on our feet".

I do not know how he managed to say Mass that evening in the tiny chapel.

We were all absolutely shattered. I felt so frustrated, as this was to have been the highlight of the tour for me.

By morning we had recovered sufficiently to visit the little 13th century chapel that St Francis and his initial Friars originally built, the Porziuncola, or little chapel of St Mary of the Angels. This is enclosed by a vast church. We then saw the actual infirmary where he died.

Another Franciscan, St Anthony, has a Basilica dedicated to him in Padua.

This is a beautiful ornate building with towers and domes. Inside were some of Donatello's masterpieces. The relics of this famous saint I found rather gruesome. They are his jaw-bone and uncorrupted tongue. Ugh! He is the saint one prays to when something is lost.

It was not long before we arrived at the outskirts of Venice at Mestre and our hotel.

"Who's coming to explore?" asked Terry after we had enjoyed our evening meal.

It was dusk and still fairly early.

A group of about six of us ventured into the unknown. In the distance we could hear music. It was like a magnet. Louder and louder the nearer we got, until we turned a corner and there, in the Piazzo Ferretto was a fiesta in full swing.

There were crowds of laughing folk. Musicians were playing and people dancing. It did not take long for most of our small group to join in. I happily wandered around the square looking in the windows of some of the classy shops and generally enjoying the atmosphere. I was unaware that I had caused consternation amongst our small group when they could not see me. Had I been kidnapped? We arrived back at the hotel deservedly worn out.

The following day was a long one.

We set off early to explore the fabulous city of Venice. With good reason it is said to be one of the world's most beautiful and elegant cities. It was high tide and they had put in the flood boards to give a raised walkway in St Mark's Square.

In the morning a Guide gave us a sight seeing tour, then we were free until six o'clock when we were to meet back at St Mark's.

"Don't worry," said Laura, "St Mark's Basilica is visible throughout the city and everywhere there are signs 'Per San Marco.'"

My independent spirit asserted itself and I spent a happy time alone, exploring.

It was at a time like this, when my basic Italian conversation classes were a real asset. I lunched in a bar "EVE'sdropping" a couple of fishermen trying to understand snippets of their conversation. My vocabulary was reasonable, my grammar abysmal, but I found I was able to make myself understood when bargaining for some small Venetian glass pendants. Two for the price of one!

The shopkeepers were so friendly and encouraging with my hesitant speech. They invited me into the back of the shop and showed me the small workshop where the red-hot glass was being shaped. I had not intended the tour to be a shopping spree and had limited money but being a bit eccentric, I did buy one other glass item. A fly! I could not resist it. It is a perfect life sized replica of an ordinary house fly. It certainly was easy to pack and did not cause any excess baggage weight!

I walked over many of the Bridges of the Grand Canal. The Rialto Bridge is full of fascinating shops. It is an amazing structure with symmetrical stone arches that was built in the sixteenth century.

There are over a hundred islands in Venice and I wandered over minor bridges and saw shops, offices, dwellings and more picturesque churches. I saw the famous gondolas, some obviously for tourists with the "gondolieri" dressed in traditional uniform. I also saw many gondolas being used to transport goods. It was a real education.

I marvelled at the ancient architecture as I wandered through small lanes and markets. I spent some time exploring and appreciating the dominant Basilica of St Mark's. The mosaics were breathtaking and the decorations in the dome unbelievable.

I met the others and we had an indifferent but unforgettable meal in the Piazza del San Marco at dusk. We sat outside in the balmy evening listening to romantic music being played by a group of musicians with a piano, violin, cello and accordion, just magic. What an amazing day.

In Verona we had a brief stop to see the supposed "home" of Juliet. It is a tradition that those who fondle her left breast will have good luck so one breast was dull and the other glossy. Not like "The young girl of Devizes"

> "Whose breasts were of two different sizes.
> One was so small
> It was no good at all
> But the other was huge and won prizes."

We did not stay long there but were on the road again and soon arrived at Bologna. The imposing ancient Cathedral was enormous and contained some beautiful statues and art. There were vivid decorations on the walls including some illustrations of Dante's Inferno where there were scenes of Mohammad being cast into hell. I believe this old church now has to be protected from terrorists.

The meridian line of light that beams into the centre of the church is from a hole in the roof indicating the time of day, very ingenious.

It was very wet all day and all the way to Florence. To our joy, the clouds and mist lifted as we reached the hill approaching the city and beheld a copy of the huge statue of David, a taste of things to come. Below us, clearly visible was the magnificent Renaissance city of Florence with all its treasures.

Sunday our sight seeing day was marred by the fact that the churches were not open for tourists.

It was Environment Day and no cars were allowed in the city. Hundreds of umbrellas hampered our progress as we fought our way against a sea of teenagers. We had not been aware that Florence was the venue of the Year 2000 Youth Rally. The Duomo that dominated the city was as magnificent as I expected with its huge Baptistry and intricately carved "Door of Paradise".

We admired the statue of Neptune and of course the famous one of young David and other statues in the Piazza della Signore.

The queue for the lavatories, in this city was the worst we experienced, probably because of the excessive crowds, and I was pretty desperate by the time I made it. Those continental ones where one squats really disconcert me.

Then, I had a very different experience from the rest of the group as we had a free afternoon. Don's cousin Linda had married a Florentine doctor many years previously and she planned to meet me.

There were no cars that day, so we took a taxi to their delightful large apartment. He has his consulting room there, it looked like a real old fashioned doctor's surgery with a mahogany desk and a couple of comfortable leather chairs.

Here I met Enrico again. They had visited Australia briefly some years ago.

Their antique furniture looked perfect in those rooms with very high ceilings.

After lunch she said those magic words:

"We all have a siesta for two hours."

Oh, how I needed it and enjoyed that compulsory relaxation. Afterwards Linda and I went on the bus to the Basilica of San Miniato del Monte, up umpteen steps at the top of a hill. A real bonus was hearing the monks singing their Vespers in plainchant. Afterwards we both indulged in an ice cream. Italian ice creams are so special and delicious, I think I indulged in one each day I was in Italy, just as in France I succumbed to a daily gateau.

While Linda prepared food for dinner, Enrico took me in his new Alfa Romeo car, his pride and joy, to Fiesole, a charming place in the hills. We had magnificent yiews over Venice. Enrico speaks no English but we managed to converse a little in Italian.

Back home, after a meal of pasta, roast meat and raspberries and cream, ("saporita" — delicious) we finished with Linda's limonella liqueur, very potent.

We all watched the closing ceremony of the Olympic Games in Australia on their television. They then returned me tired but happy to the hotel.

The next day, we had a rare early start as we had a long day travelling. Pisa was crowded with tourists, but unbelievably, next to me, amongst the throngs gazing up at the famous leaning tower, were Joanne and her family who I had met on our tour of Ireland. We all agreed that the Basilica was a very peaceful and prayerful place. We also visited the huge Baptistry on this fleeting visit.

We diverted briefly for lunch in Lavagna, Laura's home town where she introduced us to her good looking twin son and daughter. Then it was off through the tunnel to emerge into France.

We looked down on to Monte Carlo from the cliffs up above the town and then headed for Nice.

I remembered the photos in our old photo album as my parents had their honeymoon there in 1921. Nothing looked very different. Palms still graced the promenade where elegant folk paraded.

In the morning we wandered among the colourful fruit and flower markets. I bought some of those unique sweets I remembered as a child, that look exactly like pebbles and taste delicious. In the Cathedral was a dramatic display of vestments.

Cannes had an atmosphere of sophistication and opulence. There were large yachts in the Marina, I saw a lot of expensive cars and I even noticed that epitome of France, a stylish lady walking her trimmed, white poodle.

The first French song I learned as a child was "Frère Jacques". The second one was "Sur le pont d' Avignon". Here I was actually on this famous bridge, surprised to only find part of it. Apparently, floods destroyed it in the 17th century and demolished eighteen of the arches, only four remain, it was never rebuilt.

The enormous gothic building of the Palace was home to seven Popes in the 14th century. I toured this vast stronghold listening to information on audio. I felt both awestruck and bewildered with so much information but it was well worth the effort of concentration.

The next day we had a very special, unscheduled treat in store. The countryside was now flat and very pretty. We came to the double walled, fortified, medieval city of Carcassonne.

This dramatic, compact town delighted me but one thing that intrigued me was the pig on the flag flying from the tower. All the shops had pig statues and I was curious, why?

I found a bookshop and saw a children's book about Carcassonne and managed to understand the story with my limited knowledge of French. How I wish now, that I had bought this little book *L'histoire de Carcassonne*.

Once upon a time, hundreds of years ago, the Saracens captured the city and lived happily alongside their French captives.

The great king Charlemagne heard that the town was under enemy rule and was determined to rescue it. He sent his army to destroy the Saracens but the double wall enclosing the city prevented any assailant entering. Meanwhile, inside, the people were becoming more anxious and thinner. They had eaten all their supplies and were unable to go out into the adjacent fields to harvest their crops or tend their cattle, because of the soldiers camped outside the walls. Then the Saracen princess had an idea.

"Bring me all the food we have left," she commanded.

Small hoards of wheat were shovelled into a sack and one person had a very thin pig.

"Feed all the grain to the pig," she said to the starving townsfolk. "Trust me." She assured them.

When the pig grew to be plump and the grain was all eaten, she threw it over the wall into the midst of Charlemagne's army.

"What are they doing, throwing fat pigs like this away?" the General mused.

"They must have such a store of food that we are wasting our time camping out here waiting for them to surrender."

He ordered his troops to depart and the townspeople rejoiced in the wisdom of their princess. They were free to continue their lives in peace and like all good stories "live happily ever after."

The flat landscape changed dramatically as we headed for the Pyrenees and Lourdes. One thing I have always disliked intensely, is what I think of as "mass hysteria". Football matches, rallies, demonstrations and even religious processions. Lourdes was a prime example of this.

Unfortunately I had been suffering from a stomach upset which also helped to dampen my enthusiasm. The town was absolutely packed with pilgrims. Later, in England, Sister Odile told me we were there the

92

week there was a big gathering of some special group from all over France. The faith of all these people was almost tangible. I found it very moving and incredibly sad, to see so many folk on stretchers and in wheelchairs during the evening candlelight procession, all hoping for a cure.

One minor bonus for me was that as the rosary was recited in French, I happily joined in as I had learned the "Hail Mary" in French at Annecy Convent in Sussex, before I knew the English version.

Everywhere there were souvenir shops all selling identical items. The whole place seemed far too commercialised, a contrast to the original site, where a simple peasant girl had a vision of Mary in a grotto in the hills in 1858. For many the visit was the highlight of the tour.

We had an early Mass in Lourdes then left for the long six hundred kilometre coach trip. Apart from lunch and a couple of necessary stops, we were travelling all that day. Thank God I had taken my travel sickness tablets!

We drove around Bordeaux but did not stop as we had to arrive in Tours in time for our meal.

Chartres Cathedral is especially amazing. It was built in the 12th century in only fifty years. The stained glass windows with their particularly vivid blues, all tell bible stories. The Rose window is awe-inspiring. The sun illuminated the ancient glass. The statues and carvings were incredibly life-like. The fascinating labyrinth with eleven circuits divided into four quadrants is on the floor of this Gothic masterpiece and was fun to try to negotiate.

Afterwards I wandered alone through the markets and side streets until I saw a Patisserie. There inside, was my very favourite gateau, a coffee éclair, how I enjoyed it.

We assembled at the coach as arranged and realised that one of our group was missing. A moment of panic but she was eventually found and re-united with the rest of us.

As we approached Paris, the traffic became more and more concentrated but we soon arrived at our hotel on the outskirts, unfortunately in a heavy downpour.

The rain continued nearly all the short time we had in this magic city, a pity.

After our meal we said goodbye to our driver Bruno and Laura as they were returning to Italy with the coach, but not before our final sortie, Paris at night.

We saw the illuminated Eiffel tower and floodlit Notre Dame Cathedral all through a haze of rain. The huge Millennium Wheel dominated the skyline.

We then queued in the rain, to push our way on to the large boat for our trip under the twenty two bridges that cross the Seine. It must have held over a hundred people and we were squashed like sardines.

"Look," said Betty. "There are seats over there." I squeezed my way along the row to get a seat at the edge. It was all open but there was an awning overhead to keep us dry. Alas, I sat down in a large puddle. That is why that seat had been unoccupied. The rain had blown in, but by then I was trapped. I finished the trip

94

in considerable discomfort with soaking trousers and wet knickers. Quite an exhausting day!

The final day we had a Guide on the Cityrama coach. We ascended to the first stage of the Eiffel Tower and were given an excellent commentary on the many famous and historical landmarks.

As in Florence, it was our misfortune to be there on a Sunday when tourists were not taken to the magnificent Notre Dame Cathedral. I was so pleased I had been given the opportunity some years ago to attend Mass there, an unforgettable experience.

We finished at the Louvre. I had visited this splendid Gallery before. I was surprised and shocked that about half of the group decided to return to the hotel to rest and pack, as tomorrow we were departing.

I could not bear to waste half a day in Paris in spite of the sheeting rain. Father Tony, Terry, Shelagh and I decided to explore together. Father Tony had always wanted to walk along the Champs Élyssées to the Arc de Triomphe.

I found my limited knowledge of the French language very useful as no one else on the tour spoke any. We saw the tomb of the Unknown Soldier from the First World War and the Eternal Flame. We then took the Metro to Sacré Coeur, the enormous imposing Basilica crowning the hill of Mont Martre.

Terry and Father Tony, young and fit, walked up the long flight of steep steps. Shelagh and I knew our limitations and happily took the Funicular. Sacré Coeur was in the process of restoration and it was still raining but our spirits were not dampened. We decided to meet at the steps in a couple of hours.

I happily strolled through the magical streets of Mont Martre. I listened to singers and buskers, watched artists at work in the little lanes and generally soaked up the ambience of this captivating place.

We met for a meal just as the sun shone for a short while.

Father Tony was able to achieve his romantic ambition of seeing the sun set over Paris.

By the time we had descended the steps, caught the Metro and had a fair walk back to the hotel, I was totally exhausted. Terry just about carried me.

The final morning most of us took the bus to Gare Nord to catch Eurostar to England. I had always wanted the experience of travelling on this train beneath the Channel.

Everyone else caught the train early in the morning as they were going to London, but as I was alighting at Ashford in Kent, I had longer to wait for mine. The journey was very smooth and a fitting end to the Pilgrimage.

My holiday was not yet finished. Bill, Don's niece Valerie's husband met me at Ashford and drove me through pretty villages to their home in Sittingbourne.

They had always been dear and faithful friends of mine. We spent a few days sightseeing locally including the historical city of Canterbury.

He then drove me to Surrey to see Don's sister Win. She was very independent at eighty eight and still lived alone. It was not far to Veronica's house where I spent a couple of days.

"Anywhere special you would like to visit?" she asked me.

"David has time off work and will happily drive you."

I had one definite request.

"I would love to visit Seaford on the South Coast and see dear Sister Brigid again."

Veronica and David kindly took me there the following day and whilst they explored the town, I spent a couple of treasured hours with her and the other three elderly nuns, happily chatting and reminiscing. They are so proud that Penelope Keith had been a boarder there for many years. I remembered tucking her up in bed, as a dear little girl, when I was a "big girl".

On October 14th, the day of my departure, Veronica drove me a short distance to Effingham to see Don's nephew Stephen and his partner Alison. We had lunch in a typically old English pub with oak beams and then we went to Guildford for a sentimental drive around the city.

We found the house where I used to babysit Stephen and Valerie in 1952.

"Don't watch me take my vest off. Its *rude*." I could happily bathe him!

His was the first car I have been in with heated seats. Sam their Old English Sheepdog sat in the back of the Volvo as we drove to Heathrow. Here I met some of the other pilgrims who were returning that day. Some had other plans.

As I walked through the security gate I heard a loud "beep beep". They questioned me in detail and I entered again.

"Empty your pockets," demanded the rather aggressive Indian lady official.

I did so. "Beep beep" continued.

We finally discovered the culprit. I was wearing a metal badge saying:

"Be nice to me, it is my birthday."

She did have the grace to be as amused as I was and I proceeded into the Airport for the inevitable, interminable waiting around and then — the long journey home.

A different way to spend my seventieth birthday.

CHAPTER
TEN

Here and there

To Kalgoorlie, Leonora and Esperance by train.
Lovely South West holidays and wildflower terrain.

I have been on many overseas holidays since retirement but have also enjoyed a variety of lesser tours and holidays within Western Australia.

Some years ago I was enjoying a meal out with a group of friends. One of their members had moved to Albany a few years previously and she joined us on this particular occasion.

"I don't know Albany," I said "Are you happy there?"

"We love it, you'll have to come and stay with us."

This invitation from a stranger intrigued me. I asked Erica, "Did Shirley mean it when she issued that invitation?"

"Shirley would never say anything she didn't mean." assured Erica.

Later that year I contacted her and spent an enjoyable few days in February as their guest in their lovely home. It is always considerably cooler in Albany than Perth as it is about 380 km south of Armadale. I travelled there on the bus and Shirley and Jim kindly took me to see some of the many attractions in the area. I visited them a few times and each time saw something new.

Once Annette accompanied me and once Gillian and I stayed independently and visited Shirley but did our own sightseeing. That was when we went to the Wind Farm and I gazed in awe at the twelve, huge turbine generators that were sixty five metres high.

The first day they took me for a drive to the top of Mt Clarence. Below us was the magic vista of the Southern Ocean and the large natural port of King George Sound.

This is always busy with ships loading wood and other goods for export. Near the summit is a nine metre high statue — a memorial to the Desert Mounted Corps who left with the original Anzacs in 1914 for World War I.

On another occasion we went to the top of Mt Adelaide where the Princess Royal fortress presides over a fascinating Army Museum of memorabilia and an old building housing the tea rooms. As we drove along the coast I gasped at the magnificent deserted beaches of golden sand and azure water.

I love the town itself, centred in the main York Street. There is some interesting old architecture. We went into the elegant Town Hall and St John's Church also the old Gaol that has many spellbinding legends. Often at my request, Shirley would leave me for an hour or so to wander and pick me up later.

Once, when alone, my bladder called. I cannot ignore it and looked around hopefully but all I saw was a Seniors Centre. "Aha" I thought, "There is bound to be a lavatory there." And of course I was right. As I emerged, I saw groups of men and women around tables earnestly playing some game with letter tiles.

"What are you playing?" I asked.

"Rummikub." Came the terse reply.

This started my love affair with this fascinating game which is a form of Rummy but uses strategy as well as luck. For years before she left for England, we played with Alison and Frank. We now play fortnightly with Gillian and Erica.

Shirley introduced me to a friend one day as we stopped for coffee in the town. We were reminiscing and laughing about the previous evening. Shirley and I had been to a Chinese restaurant, talking about memories of Danny Kaye. We had burst into song simultaneously, with;

"I'm Anatole of Paris, the hats I sell, make
    'usbands yell,
Is that an 'at or a two roomed flat?
Let me get my paw on a little piece of straw,
And voilá, un chapeau, at sixty bucks a throw."

Linda told us how gullible she was as a teenager, when she bought a bottle of Tommy Steele's bath water!

I also joined Shirley a couple of times, as a guest at her local Probus meeting.

Until 1978, Humpback whales were hunted from Albany, but now the old Whaling Station is an interesting Museum called Whale World. Here I learned about the history and techniques of the industry.

Torndinnup National Park has some unusual sights. We were lucky enough to have the tide right to enable us to see the blowholes in action. When really big waves force their way through the granite rocks, water spurts up into the air. We also saw "The Gap" another formation in the rocks with a self-explanatory title.

The National Trust treasure in Albany, Strawberry Hill Farm, dates back to 1830 and as well as the interesting buildings, has really beautiful grounds. Annette and I enjoyed a Devonshire tea in these gardens but were unlucky enough to be there whilst the lawns were being mowed by an incredibly noisy machine.

Another outing was near Mt Barker some distance from the town. Here is the thriving business of Mt Romance. Emu oil products, Sandalwood goods and other merchandise is for sale in sophisticated surroundings.

They also took me to beautiful Denmark, Walpole and the Stirling Ranges.

I think what made the biggest impression on me was Edith. This amazingly talented Austrian lady and her husband Bill, retired to a beautiful home overlooking the bay in Albany. Their hobby was making dolls houses.

The quantity increased each time I visited them. They did not charge to see the display in their large garage, but one gave a donation to, I think, the

Lifesaving Society. Shirley phoned her to see when it would be convenient for us to visit her.

These houses, of all types, are exquisite in their detail. Bill makes the actual buildings and Edith furnishes them and even makes the realistic looking inhabitants.

There were family homes, a large assortment of shops, a school, a church, a hospital, a castle, an art gallery, a "mouse house" and many, many more. There was even a brothel. The leer on one of the men's faces was so lifelike.

Once I was chatting to her about the construction of an item.

"Did you make that with Fimo?" I asked. She was delighted I knew of this modelling material.

"Come inside." She invited us.

Shirley had longed to see inside the house so was delighted to accept the offer.

I think everything, except the packet of biscuits had been hand made; the curtains, the ceramic cups and saucers, the paintings on the walls, the soft furnishings, the ornaments and possibly Bill had made the furniture. She showed us some magnificent quilts she had made. I think she was one of the most talented ladies I have ever met.

The most intriguing thing about her was the story of her life and how she came to Western Australia from Austria. One incident she related was when they were being sent by train to a camp at Northam, soon after the end of the war. On the stations as they passed, they saw people waving their hands and thought what a friendly place this was. Only later did she realise that they were brushing away the flies!

I could have stayed all day listening to her and also admiring those fabulous dolls houses.

Another occasion that I will always remember was a rail holiday to Kalgoorlie, Leonora and Esperance. Rail travel has always been my favourite and on this holiday I did not go alone but with my dear friend Mary.

This adventure was on a privately chartered "Prospector" train that travels from Perth to Kalgoorlie. This long nine hour, tedious journey where I got a numb bum! was relieved by having the rare treat of good company.

A bus met us and deposited us at our motel. That evening, we had a bus tour of the town which was very quiet, as it was Saturday and were also shown Hay Street, the famous red light district.

The next day was extremely hot as it tends to be in that area. We took the train 230 km east to Leonora.

> Said a cheeky girl from Leonora
> Whose boy was beginning to bore her:
> "Do you mean birds and bees
> Go through antics like these
> To provide us with flora and fauna?"

I was very impressed with the beautifully restored old buildings in the town. Some we saw, were built from corrugated iron and hessian, materials that were easy to transport to this isolated area.

At the ghost town of Gwalia, we saw the large open pit and the restored huge Oregon headframe and steam winding engine. These massive constructions dominate the small museum that was very interesting. We also wandered through an old camp that had been restored but we were not given enough time for me to satisfy my curiosity about so many things.

Early the next morning before catching the train to Esperance we had a quick look at the Super Pit. It was absolutely enormous. Apparently it is as deep as Uluru (Ayers Rock) is high. It produces over 800,000 ounces of gold a year and is the biggest open-cut gold mine in Australia.

It was a long journey from Kalgoorlie and we stopped for lunch near Norseman. Here a group of C.W.A. ladies had prepared a lunch of real damper and billy tea for us. We had delicious Tate and Lyle's golden syrup with it, to my surprise. The scenery consisted of a lot of scrub and salt lakes, pretty desolate.

It happened to be Melbourne Cup day, so we had a sweep on the train. Mary got two horses but won nothing.

We arrived in Esperance early in the evening. Whilst in Kalgoorlie we had shared our dining table with some rather dreary folk, so I suggested that here we go to the dining room early, get seated and see who joins us.

It turned out to be an excellent idea, as Norman and Hazel came, a delightful older couple who were celebrating their third wedding anniversary that weekend. Not only did we enjoy their company for the last days of the tour but have stayed in touch since and meet occasionally.

The next morning we all went to the jetty and boarded the catamaran *Sea Breeze*.

Mary just loved it but in spite of taking my tablets I felt distinctly queasy and was happy I did not disgrace myself. Although it was a bright sunny day, the sea was definitely choppy. We saw some seals basking on one of the many islands.

Afterwards, too soon afterwards for me, we went for a bus tour around some beautiful bays. The sea was bright blue and the sand looked almost white.

In contrast, we were taken to a huge salt lake that appeared to be pink. Apparently this is due to the number of red algae in the water. Unfortunately I had to rest for a while in the afternoon but after that, I had quite recovered. I was foolish to go in a boat, but I hate to miss anything.

We had a quick look around the shops in the town and in the evening we went to the Pier Hotel for a banquet and sat happily with our new-found friends.

Back on the train we went the following day, for the long trip back to Kalgoorlie. This time we were given a boxed salad lunch whilst on the journey. It always surprises me how tired one gets just travelling.

We arrived at our hotel in Kalgoorlie and had a pleasant dinner before an early night.

Our final morning again was oppressively hot. The four of us shared a taxi into the town of Kalgoorlie for a quick look around before boarding the train for the long, long dreary trip back. We left at 9.35a.m. and arrived in Perth on time at 6.05pm and then had to catch two more trains to return us to Armadale.

I had enjoyed the company of Mary, Norman and Hazel but unfortunately a lot of the holiday had been spent on those necessary, time-consuming train journeys. To think I actually like rail travel, these long monotonous journeys have not really disillusioned me. Still, I had seen and enjoyed a few new locations and experiences.

Since retirement I have also taken a number of tours with a coach company that really looks after us well. Some of the places I have visited in the South West have been particularly memorable.

There are some magnificent thriving wineries in the area that we visit. I just enjoy the ambience as I am not a wine drinker. The gardens are always beautiful and of course many of the other tourists are tempted to leave laden with bottles. We visited a Lavender Farm where not only did we see quantities of lavender being grown but we indulged in delicious lavender scones with our coffee.

The Eagles Sanctuary was educational as well as entertaining. There were many raptors in cages and we had a dramatic demonstration of free flying kites swooping to catch food in mid air.

Most of these four or five day holidays I take alone, but once I went with Mary for a "Christmas in July" weekend where we stayed at the company's Villa.

We had some interesting tours around Busselton and on Saturday evening *the* dinner. I wore a polyester/ elastane top that was very stretchy. The dining room had Christmas decorations and there were balloons on each table. I don't drink and was stone cold sober but relaxed in good company. Fooling around, I put two balloons up my yielding top to the amusement of the folk around me.

Our host, the owner of the company Troy, was delighted with my tomfoolery and picked me up as if I was a feather, (and I am no featherweight) and threw me over his shoulder, galloping around the room without bursting the balloons, an unforgettable incident.

Recently I had a few days break with my friend Doth. On that tour we visited the Wardan Centre and were given an excellent display by a group of Aborigines dancing. They were painted traditionally and carried spears. One was an expert with the didgeridoo.

That afternoon we watched a Border Collie and Kelpie herd sheep at a display at Yallingup shearing shed. This is a commercial enterprise with the inevitable shop.

Before returning to the Villa we had a brief but delicious stop at the Chocolate Factory where many of us succumbed.

I always enjoy seeing the beautiful beach at Meelup.

Then we visited the now thriving, rather sophisticated town of Dunsborough which was just a small place when we arrived in Western Australia early in 1969.

Walpole is on the Inlet and we had a trip on the river with an excellent local commentator who was very informative and entertaining. Near here is the Valley of the Giants Tree Top Walk. This refers to the Tingle forest, some of the most massive trees in the world. I have made this walk twice and each time I found it thrilling as we actually meandered through the canopy of these huge trees. I also took the walk through the veteran trees at ground level.

Western Australia is known as the Wildflower State with good reason. There are over twelve thousand species, many of them unique to the West. I took a short wildflower tour of the South West, as I had always wanted to visit Wave Rock and this formed part of the itinerary.

We headed for Albany to stay in a motel there. We had a few hours free so I caught up with Shirley and Jim briefly. We were lucky enough to have a very knowledgeable driver who had lived in the area. She was able to point out numerous interesting features along the way and many of the wildflowers.

Inger did not try to blind us with science although she knew the correct name of most of the species. All I can remember is "Anigozanthos manglesii", the name of the common kangaroo paw, the floral emblem of Western Australia. We saw many of these and also the carnivorous plant that thrives locally.

The next day we went to the Banksia Farm at Mt Barker. I had feared this might prove to be a bit boring, far from it, I was entranced. There were over seventy seven species of banksias and even more dryandras. Kevin gave us an intriguing talk and my only complaint was that we were not there long enough. It was the time of year that we were able to appreciate the magnificent wildflower garden that they have nurtured. There were quantities of everlastings, hakeas, grevillias and many, many more.

Bluff Knoll is the highest peak in the Stirling Range mountains and our destination another day. We drove through the Porongorup National Park. Here there was a profusion of wildflowers and many species of orchids for the connoisseurs.

Inger told us of a local tree with the lovely name of "Snottygobble". I felt very emotional at Bluff Knoll as Oliver had been hiking here many times when he lived "in the West".

We lunched at The Lily, a working replica of a Dutch windmill from 1600 A.D.., isolated high on the hill, with a house nearby and a very good restaurant.

That night we spent at Bremer Bay and then had morning tea the next day at Warramungup, what a lovely name.

We passed through Ravensthorpe which was like a ghost town on a Sunday, then past the salt lake at Lake King until we reached Hyden. Yellow cassias and other colourful flowers bordered the roadside.

This was the Public Holiday weekend for the Queen's Birthday and aptly at Wave Rock, they held a Rock Festival. Our motel was far enough out of town not to be disturbed by them during the evening.

The following morning when we arrived at the Rock, there were umpteen tents scattered beneath it with a variety of bleary eyed individuals, emerging from them. Some had dreadlocks, some dressed in outlandish garments, others surprisingly conventional. None were troublesome or offensive and waved cheerily at us as we reached for our cameras to take photos of this multi-coloured granite rock that resembles a giant surf wave.

I feared that I might be disappointed when I actually viewed it but I certainly was not. The size, over seventy seven metres high had me awe struck.

The red, yellow and grey colours are said to change according to the time of day but we only saw it in the morning, which thankfully was fine.

Wildflowers abounded in the area and we saw the beautiful bright blue leschenaultia, verticordias, firebush and lots of donkey and spider orchids. Western Australia has very strict rules that no wildflowers may be picked without a special licence.

The Wildflower shop at Hyden was a fascinating place. All I could see of the wildflowers for sale, were either dried ones or packets of seeds but there were many other fascinating items in this large shop.

Adjacent is the Lace Shop. This is like a museum and has a comprehensive collection of lace and chests of drawers containing samples from all over the world. There were wedding dresses displayed and at the entrance a copy of the painting of my friend, *The Laughing Cavalier* with his lace collar. I refer to him as "my friend", because in my childhood, we lived just around the corner from the Wallace Collection in Central London where the original Franz Hals painting is displayed. His eyes follow you all around the room.

Later that day we travelled through more interesting small towns and saw more prolific flowers in the bush

111

on the way home. I realised that we had only seen a few of the enormous number and variety of wildflowers in Western Australia.

What a State to be in!

CHAPTER
ELEVEN

President and Floriade
2001

A happy trip to Canberra and Probus Rendezvous.
Floriade, balloon flight and Telstra Tower view.

I had joined the Trefoil Guild and asked Merle if we would be having some outings.

She suggested I join Probus and with her kind introduction, I did just that.

I enjoyed the new status of being a Probian and making many new friends.

Each month we had an interesting speaker, but the big attraction for me was the following week, when we went on a coach tour.

We had many interesting venues and saw outlying towns that I had only heard of and would never have visited otherwise. This was just what I wanted. Don has never liked to drive to new places and my knowledge of the more remote places was nil.

For many happy years my horizons widened, as did my eyes.

Some years after joining, I found to my horror that I was to become President. This was a huge ordeal for me. My lot in life has always been to be a follower, not a leader.

By the end of the year, I realised I had coped without any major trauma but was quite happy to pass on the responsibility to my successor.

During that year I attended the National Probus Rendezvous in Canberra for all the Australia and New Zealand Clubs. I chose to fly there and joined the West Australian members who had crossed Australia by coach. Air travel was an excellent option for me as I dislike long coach journeys. The coach company had planned an exciting itinerary around the Rendezvous commitments.

The band from the Duntroon Army Cadets and U.3.A choir opened the seminar. We had some excellent speakers and spent a while socialising with our hosts. I was delighted to find an old friend and colleague from Western Australia there. Ann moved to Canberra some years before to be near her daughter.

I hoped my long held ambition for a hot air balloon flight was to be realised on this holiday. The first day was cancelled because of the weather. The second day we were there at dawn and helped unroll and inflate the huge balloon but then it was cancelled again due to the weather, very disappointing. Third time lucky. A car collected me at 5.00a.m. The temperature was 0°C and it was cold and frosty, but a clear morning and perfect for the flight. The experience exceeded all my expectations. We glided over so many famous landmarks, the War Memorial. New Parliament House, various embassies and skimmed over Lake Burley Griffin.

All the time a four wheel drive vehicle was following our progress on the ground. Geoff our "driver" was in constant radio contact. When we finally landed and had to vacate the huge basket that had carried us, I was unable to climb out.

My exit was most undignified as I had to be lifted out bodily, by short, but obviously very strong, Geoff. How humiliating! However, it was a lifetime's ambition achieved.

Clinton, our young coach driver, gave us a comprehensive tour of the interesting embassies, many built in the style of the country they represented.

We then visited New Parliament House and the Australian Museum, all too briefly.

I had not known that the War Memorial was a lot more than the name implies.

This beautiful landmark is of Byzantine design and in an impressive position at the foot of Mount Ainslie. It is a fascinating was museum. There we saw the Tomb of the Unknown Soldier surrounded by four huge stained glass windows. Many aspects of various wars are graphically displayed. The one that (literally) moved me most, was the "live" display of Bomber Command in action. Here I stood in a claustrophobic replica of a Lancaster bomber feeling the vibrations and hearing the gunfire and very realistic dropping of the bombs. It gave me a little idea of some of Don's wartime ordeals.

115

A very moving, unforgettable, grim photo was of an Australian soldier, head bowed, about to be beheaded by a Japanese soldier. I wondered what the hoards of Japanese tourists that flocked there thought. I found it a very interesting but rather depressing place as "war" is all too vivid in my memory.

The following day we visited the breathtaking tulip gardens. The weather and setting were perfect as were the blooms.

We then returned to Canberra for a couple of hours. After a hasty lunch I spent my time exploring and found a unique shop that sold amongst other intriguing things, pig and wolf masks. Doubtless I will explain my need for these in another chapter.

As we had various options for the afternoon, I alone chose to spend a couple of fascinating hours at "Questacon", the National Science and Technology centre.

It was full of groups of children all revelling in the many interactive exhibits. I loved them too, (the exhibits, not necessarily the noisy, excited children!) I experienced caged lightning and hid in a shelter for a very realistic encounter with a cyclone — pretty terrifying!

I had a wait for the coach and was browsing through all the temptations in the Museum shop when I got carried away with extravagance, after all, I was on holiday.

I bought an unusual musical kaleidoscope to add to my collection.

That evening Ann collected me and took me up to the summit on the Black Mountains to the famous Telstra Tower. We went up to the viewing platform and had a 360 degree night-time vista all around Canberra. This was a real bonus and very kind of her.

I was pretty tired the next morning after my early but successful balloon adventure.

We headed for the Royal Australian Mint. I had visited the Mint in Perth and this is the only other coin producing Mint in Australia. We watched a relevant video and saw a comprehensive display of minted coins. It did not delight me as much as the Mint in Perth, as we did not have the opportunity to actually see gold poured, a literally dazzling sight.

It was the time of year when Canberra was celebrating its annual Floriade.

Commonwealth Park was transformed with over a million bulbs and blooms, quite spellbinding. The weather was perfect. The vibrant colours of the tulips and other bright spring flowers had me hunting in my bag for my new camera.

I was bending down to take a close-up photo, when I felt a tap on my shoulder. It was John and his wife Anne who were visiting one of their sons who lived in Canberra. They lived just up the hill from me in Armadale and we were all members of our local U.3.A. What a coincidence. I enjoyed chatting to them and enthused about all I had seen.

"Have you been to Tittington Green?" asked John

"No," I replied, "Tell me about it."

"It is a really wonderful miniature village." he replied.

"Oh, do you mean Cockington Green?" I asked. A pregnant pause followed, then a laugh.

"Well. I knew the name involved something rude!" he said.

I have never let him forget this remark and now I have to stop and think what the village is actually called.

We had been there the previous day and I was entranced. Years ago I had visited Madurodam in Holland famed for its miniature village but I definitely preferred Cockington Green. The layout was really spacious and the houses perfect replicas. They were based on English buildings, inns, churches, cottages and mansions all with imaginative and colourful landscaping.

The big bonus for me was the model railway that ran around the grounds. I spent a happy time mystifying some of the visitors who were not aware that I was at the controls. I have always loved train sets of any size. I think it stems from my childhood, coveting the one that belonged to my big brothers that I was not allowed to touch. I loved Cockington Green.

The final evening Probus had a Gala Dinner at old Parliament House, a very imposing building. Here, Margaret Reid, the first woman president of the Australian Senate, gave an interesting if rather lengthy speech after the meal.

We all met at the aptly named Convention Centre for the finale of the convention. There were more impressive choirs singing and inevitable speeches.

I said goodbye to my new-found Rendezvous friends and thanked Ann for her guidance and company.

My memories of Canberra will be dominated by the voices of the melodious choirs, the brilliance of Floriade, my balloon flight, the moving experience of the War Memorial and of course Tittington, no sorry! Cockington Green.

CHAPTER
TWELVE

Priests and Penguins 2002

We toured with Father Tony for his Silver Jubilee.
To Adelaide, excursions too and Glenelg-by-the-Sea.

Father Tony had attended a Seminary in Adelaide to train for the priesthood.

It was soon to be his Silver Jubilee so he and Bishop Don Sproxton intended joining their colleague Father Gauchi from Adelaide there, for a special celebration.

Our Parish had enjoyed the 2000 Pilgrimage and decided to help them commemorate this event in November.

A mere three hour flight on Virgin Airlines and we were in Adelaide. We found the flight attendants courteous and attractive. The seats were adequate but not luxurious.

We settled into our hotel and after lunch our driver Phil who was also a parishioner, took us on an orientation tour of the city. It was an extremely hot day, 38°C.

The following day we had some wine tasting, but not for me. Still, I enjoyed the visits to the invariably attractive buildings in pleasant settings.

On the way to Victor Harbour, I saw the most massive Moreton Bay Fig tree I have ever seen. These magnificent trees remind me a little of the stately cedars one sees in England.

After Victor Harbour, we had a long drive to see the impressive Mouth of the Murray River.

A horse-drawn tram took us down the jetty to cross to Granite Island. We watched a film of the little penguins that live there, followed by an actual procession of them as they came ashore at twilight. We were told no torches were allowed as they might become disoriented.

Adelaide is a compact, fascinating city about the same size as Perth. One thing that really enchanted me was the various bronze figures scattered throughout the Shopping Precinct. I loved the realistic pig looking into the litter bin.

Hahndorf, in the hills outside Adelaide is named after the Danish sea captain who brought the German immigrants to the area in 1838. The oppressed Lutherans were able to worship freely here. The traditional German architecture is complimented by the many restaurants with German cuisine. I enjoyed browsing through some of the many small art galleries and shops.

Adelaide's old railway station has been converted to the Sky City Casino, a very impressive venue where we enjoyed a delicious meal. I quickly lost the small

121

amount of money I had allotted for this venture, and enjoyed watching the perseverance of those who optimistically fed endless coins into the machines. I lack a gambling instinct.

More wineries to visit. Many of these had been established by German immigrants. The tastings delighted many of the group. We then headed through the rolling hills, pretty townships and manicured vineyards of the Barossa Valley to the Whispering Wall. The Dam here was completed in 1903 and is the biggest one in Australia. The walls are ten metres thick at the base and taper upwards to a pathway along the top.

This parabolic, curved concrete wall bounces the sound off with an amazing effect. These acoustics are astonishing. A whisper can be heard the other side, over a hundred metres distant. We had a most impressive tour of the huge Seppelts winery. We then had lunch at another winery that had an extensive gift shop. There I bought myself a unique scarf ring. It is made of tiny gumnuts and leaves, copper plated. This attractive item reminds me of my holiday whenever I wear it and always attracts comments.

A small diversion followed as we stopped on our way home, to see a man with twenty eight dogs giving an obedience demonstration. I was impressed with them but felt they looked decidedly scruffy. How I missed my little dog, but doubtless Don was caring for her adequately.

On Friday we headed for the Riverlands District and the Murray River for a cruise on "The Proud Mary".

This luxurious boat took us for an all too short but enjoyable trip. We travelled through to Torrens Gorge. On the way back to our hotel, we stopped at Gumeracha where there was a grotesque, huge rocking horse on the roadway advertising the toy factory. We bought refreshments and had a look around the extensive and expensive display.

I was really glad I had taken my excellent, long lasting, effective travel sickness tablets that day. The drive home was through the spectacular countryside of the Mount Lofty ranges but with many winding roads and lanes.

Saturday morning was free, so I took myself to the city centre and happily looked around Rundle Street and managed to find a craft shop to browse through.

Our lunch that day was a progressive one, starting with Irish fare at Brecknocks. We then all boarded the tram for the bumpy ride to the place with the palindromic name, Glenelg-on-Sea for dessert and coffee.

> When I visited Glenelg-on-Sea,
> I invited the Duchess to tea.
> Her rumblings abdominal
> Were really phenomenal,
> And everyone thought it was me.

I enjoyed wandering around this thriving, busy seaside resort with very old, interesting buildings.

We returned for an hour or so to the hotel to get dressed up for the big event, then back to Glenelg.

Here, we had a superb meal in the Revolving Restaurant with panoramic views over the ocean, town and countryside. I was surprised and honoured to be seated at the same table as the priests. They were all very charming and convivial.

The day of the celebration of the Silver Jubilee dawned. Each hour it grew hotter and hotter and by the time we had reached the church of St Luke's at Port Noarlunga it was scorching. The Mass was held outside because of the numbers. The sermon reminded me of advice once given to clergy.

"Have a riveting introduction and a memorable ending and keep the two as close together as possible!"

Yes, a short powerful homily, then some charming liturgical dancing completed the celebratory Mass.

After a buffet lunch we enjoyed an unusual concert. Oriental dancers gyrated across horizontal bamboo poles and Philippino girls danced in colourful costumes and hats.

After all this excitement, we were happy to return to the comfort of our air conditioned hotel rooms.

On our final day after we had breakfasted and packed, we went on the coach to visit "Penola" the home of Blessed Mary MacKillop in the nineteenth century where she founded the Sisters of St Joseph.

We were shown details of her educational and welfare work, and saw the museum full of memorabilia. I strolled through the peaceful gardens and into the chapel to admire her statue there.

After a brief stop in the city it was off to the airport for the flight home.

Two memorable bits of trivia:

It was during this trip that it was mentioned how many "wet" words begin with "sp".

Splish, splash, splosh, spit, spurt, spill, splutter, splash, spume, spray, sperm, spigot, spout, sprinkle, sputum and spew.

The other story was of the man who put up a "suppository shed".

"A suppository shed?"

"Yes, he put it up himself!!"

CHAPTER
THIRTEEN

Up the "Eye" and down the mine 2002

A lively tour, the village fête, adventures unforeseen.
To Hereford then London and portraits of the Queen.

Another visit to England and dear Maureen and Paddy valiantly drove to Heathrow to meet me. My first task was to see if I could book a week's tour — anywhere, as long as it left from Worcester. I had seen coaches with a large W.A. blazoned on the side. Of course my first thought is "Western Australia" but no, it was for the large coach company Wallace Arnold.

The only tour available was to Northumbria so I booked it and sighed with relief that at least I could explore somewhere I had never been before.

First I had a pleasant week with Paddy and Maureen. One day I spent happily wandering around Worcester alone. Another day Paddy, Maureen, Michael (Paddy's twin), and Jill and I went to Hampton Court Gardens at Leominster. I knew the original Hampton Court in Surrey very well and this was also a delight. They had a mediaeval garden and a maze that I nearly got lost in. There were a lot of attractive water features but it was a pity it was between seasons as the gardens were not at their best. I enjoyed seeing their thriving kitchen garden and we had lunch in the impressive Orangery.

Maureen helped regularly at Grimley Primary School nearby. That week, they were having big celebrations for the Queen's Golden Jubilee. I watched them perform some charming country dances and let off coloured helium balloons. It was a small country school with only about 70 pupils and a delight to visit.

The Barber Institute of Fine Arts at Birmingham University was having special festivities that week. As Jill and Maureen are volunteers there, they were on duty and I happily accompanied them. The weather was gorgeous, the atmosphere relaxed and families and students all seemed to be having a great time. Stories were told about the paintings and there were many hands-on activities. I decorated an "Egyptian" bowl with acrylic paints. And lots of children were working on a large mosaic downstairs.

I had "EVE DAY" in hieroglyphics put on a bracelet, the advantage of having a short name.

On Sunday, Paddy took me for a walk down the lane to Monkwood. What a treat for me. One of the things I miss most is the English woods. There were lots of butterflies and also the dragonflies that are Paddy's particular interest.

Maureen kindly took me to the pick-up point near Worcester for the coach trip. Feeder buses collected us from different areas for the Wallace Arnold coach to drive us along the Motorway to Tynemouth. I noticed signs by the side of the road announcing: "This is Catherine Cookson Country". This famous, prolific, popular author of family sagas was born and bred in Northumbria.

Our first day there everything was closed for the Queen's Golden Jubilee holiday. I walked to the eleventh century Tynemouth Priory and saw the remains of the castle and the 15th century Chantry with its beautiful stained glass rose window and vaulted ceiling.

Now what was I going to do? I wandered into the silent town and did find a pleasant little tearoom open. My tea was served in bone china cups by a charming lady. I asked her advice on how to spend the day. She suggested a train trip to Newcastle, not far away.

There were plenty of people here and I walked past the huge statue of Earl Grey down to the Tyne Bridge. I did not venture far but did see the new Millennium Gateshead Bridge which looked surprisingly flimsy in comparison to the original Tyne Bridge.

That evening in the solitude of my bedroom, I watched the Golden Jubilee procession and celebrations on my television. Later that night, I could not sleep so thought I would switch it on again, hopefully to find an interesting, soporific programme. I was pretty surprised to find most channels showing explicit pornography.

In the morning, our first stop was the very impressive Bamburg Castle. It is the oldest inhabited castle in

128

England and dates from 630 A.D.. It was full of beautiful furniture and artefacts.

We stopped for lunch at a place with the unusual name of Seahouses. On the way to Lindisfarne, we could see Alnwick Castle (pronounced "Annick") in the distance. This is where they made the first film of "Harry Potter".

It was pouring with rain when we reached the Holy Island and we were free for a couple of hours. I wandered down a street and saw a sign saying "St Vincent de Paul." My curiosity got the better of me and I walked into the building to be greeted warmly, especially when I told them I was an S.V.P. conference member from Australia. The ladies there were hosting a camp for children. They welcomed me with a cup of tea and Sister Josepha told me stories about Saints Aidan and Cuthbert, very interesting.

I had time for a short visit to the Museum where they had a very good interactive display.

The next day we had a real treat of a visit to the city of Durham with its lovely old cobbled streets. I had a leisurely look around the magnificent Cathedral of St Oswald one of the finest Romanesque churches in England. I think it was the most beautiful one I have seen with a really spiritual atmosphere. St Bede and St Cuthbert were buried here and I think the guide told me that they also had St Oswald's head, but where?

Phyl, a member of our tour slipped on the cobbles and broke her ankle. She had to be hospitalised but fortunately her brother lived nearby so she was able to be taken care of.

The fascinating, popular village of Beamish was full of so many attractions I was bewildered. It has been reconstructed as a 1913 town very authentically. I actually plucked up my courage to go down a coal mine. I did not realise that the men had to stoop and almost bend double to hack the coal out of those dark narrow passages. It felt really scary.

The town was a delight. I walked until my legs said "enough". I went into the old Co-op shop with its three departments, into the printer's shop and the middle class dentist's house. This was very much like I remembered many homes of my childhood though I was not around in 1913. They were actually making sweets in the sweet shop, the way they would have done then. This was a very popular venue for groups of school children as we were all given samples. All the villagers were dressed appropriately and I found it was an enchanting as well as an educational experience.

The following morning the coach had to find the Motorway for the long drive home. I don't know how he managed, the mist was so extensive. I expect he had to use his fog lights.

Maureen was there to meet me in Worcester and take me back to their home. What chaos! The dining room was full of plants and the dining table covered with toys. They had been busy all week making preparations for the Village Jubilee Fête. I happily helped Maureen sort the toys which were priced very reasonably whilst Paddy was titivating and pricing the plants.

On Saturday Michael and Jill joined us for coffee and helped with the setting up of the stalls. The local Peace

Hall held many inside but the weather was lovely and we were happy outside with our popular toy stall. I could not resist buying a gorgeous little wire-haired terrier toy — for me!

There were the traditional stalls of White Elephant and handicrafts, cakes and home made jams, bric-a-brac and coconut shies and competitions for the children. One was trying to balance sitting on a long cylinder. We watched a troupe of excellent dancers. It was a typically English rural scene where most of the villagers knew each other. It was a very busy day and involved clearing up afterwards. I was quite exhausted with the unaccustomed effort and excitement.

On Sunday we had a nice restful day.

The next day, poor Maureen was not feeling well so they dropped me off in Worcester at the Porcelain Museum. Some of the old pieces of "Royal Worcester" were magnificent.

A side room held a "paint it yourself" area. Usually it is full of visitors and they often hold children's parties there. One buys a dinner plate and is given water colours to paint it with. I finally decided on one with a drawing of Worcester Cathedral on it and spent a happy hour there on my own painting the plate. They then sprayed it and it was mine. It now resides proudly on my sideboard.

That evening as Maureen was still unwell, I accompanied Paddy to a function and a dinner in Worcester's glorious old Guildhall. This very ornate building was constructed in 1723.

131

The next day Paddy decided to give Maureen another day to rest and took me to Hereford driving through exceptionally attractive countryside.

A small diversion was a visit to the stainless steel unisex lavatory that was free. Quite an experience The flush was automated as were the lights and taps. We each emerged giggling.

From the ridiculous to the sublime, we went to Hereford Cathedral.

This beautiful old building dates from Norman times and I found had a real tranquillity. They have a special exhibition of the Mappa Mundi. This amazing treasure is a large mediaeval map of the world on vellum created around 1300 A.D.. Superimposed on this pictorial manuscript are about 500 drawings depicting the history of mankind. The centre of the world was Jerusalem.

The other treasure in this Cathedral is the Chained Library dating from the 17th century. Some are old manuscipts from as far back as the 7th century and it contains 1444 books all chained to their shelves. These precious items are kept at a carefully controlled temperature and humidity.

We then looked around a quaint old Tudor house before returning to Maureen. She was now feeling considerably better. We had a couple of days in Wales that was not far away. One thing that amazed me was that the red poppies by the wayside and in the fields in England, are all yellow in Wales, quite surprising.

Paddy, being a keen ornithologist was eager to see the red kites in a certain area that they frequent. He achieved his ambition.

We found a two bedroomed flat to stay in at Brynifor in the old workhouse. The next day we went to Llandrindod Wells (I had a terrible job pronouncing it) and then on to Hay-on-Wye on the border of Wales and England. This quaint old Mediaeval town is a bibliophile's dream.

It has many antique shops but also nearly fifty bookshops, I could not believe it — paradise! I had to be circumspect because of the limit to the weight of my luggage. This was still more of a torture when we stopped for lunch and there were even more bookshops. I was in danger of overdosing!

The scenery on the way home was breathtaking.

The next evening "Do" (short for Dorothy) invited us to her home for supper. She now lived in the converted stable wing having sold the manor recently. She was a very graceful, vivacious elderly lady and her home echoed her elegance. Here is an interesting anecdote concerning the Manor house.

A few years ago here in Armadale, on a local Probus tour we visited a charming miniature village called Abingdon Green. The landscaping was enchanting and the many buildings were replicas of English ones. There were old churches, schools, pubs, cottages and to my surprise, the reproduction of "Sinton Manor". I recognised Do's home and photographed it.

When I showed it to Paddy he was mystified.

"That looks like Do's house," he said. "But not those trees behind it."

I explained. We showed the photo to Do who was very impressed at the accuracy.

"They have even got the details of the conservatory correct," she gasped. This Victorian house is not particularly outstanding or old, so why, of all the houses in England was this one chosen? Paddy gave me the challenge to find out. I did.

Apparently the owners were looking for a variety of architecture and saw a picture of this house for sale in a glossy magazine, whilst visiting the dentist. He copied it from that.

What an amazing coincidence.

Maureen and Paddy drove me to Surrey where I said goodbye to them and spent a few days with Don's nephew Stephen, Alison and their bouncy Old English Sheepdog, Sam. I spent a happy day with dear friend Veronica who lives nearby and caught up with all her family's news.

On Wednesday, I remembered to put a few family photos in my bag before I caught the fast train to Waterloo. I was surprised to see so many young, sophisticated ladies all wearing elaborate hats.

More bevies of these beauties were gathered under the clock at Waterloo, mostly with formally dressed escorts. The brightly coloured feathers and ornamented headgear amazed me. I met Margaret and Douglas as arranged, no hat for her, and then I realised, it was Ascot Day and they were all heading to the races in their finery.

Margaret and Douglas greeted me warmly and we went straight to the "London Eye" for which they had already booked tickets. I had seen pictures of this giant construction built to commemorate the Millennium. This huge 135 metre high wheel has 35 capsules, each holding up to 25 people. It takes half an hour to complete the circuit and moves very slowly. The wheel revolves constantly, so one enters and alights speedily. One is barely aware of movement, it is so smooth and slow.

Douglas is very knowledgeable and knows London well. He was a superb guide, pointing out obvious landmarks such as St Paul's, the Mall, Big Ben and the Houses of Parliament and others less well known. It was a lovely clear day and we could see for 40 kilometres in all directions with fabulous views. Then disaster struck!

We were three-quarters of the way around the circuit, when we stopped. A disembodied voice announced. "Ladies and gentlemen, there is no cause for alarm, bear with us a few minutes, our engineers are working on the problem."

This announcement was repeated at five minute intervals for half an hour, then the air conditioning went off. That was when I did feel slightly alarmed. Everything, including the doors, was electronically controlled, we were virtually trapped. Then the voice told us that the emergency supplies were under the central bench, bottles of water for those feeling dehydrated. The air conditioner started working and we had a repeat of the initial announcement. I flippantly said:

"Soon they'll tell us where the parachutes are."

It took three quarters of an hour until we were moving again and I was quite relieved to leap off when we reached ground level. All the same it was a wonderful experience that I would recommend to everyone.

Douglas had some tickets for the matinée at the Theatre. We crossed the Thames, hurrying as fast as we could over the Millennium Passenger Bridge, known as the "Wobbly Bridge" as initially it had many problems. Douglas knew the way to Theatreland via Charing Cross, Kingsway and Piccadilly Circus. We managed to have a quick snack before settling into our seats to enjoy the excellent farce by Michael Frayn, *Noises Off*. I laughed so much I was aching. I think I enjoyed watching members of the audience rocking with mirth, almost as much as the show.

Afterwards we were all ready for a cup of tea.

"I know where we'll go." said Douglas "Follow me."

Just around the corner, was Trafalgar Square and the National Gallery. We relaxed in the Gallery Tearooms enjoying our cup of tea and showing each other photos of children and grandchildren then I caught up with the local gossip. Margaret and I had met initially many, many years ago when we pushed our prams to the local Baby Clinic together. Refreshed both physically and emotionally we spent a couple of happy hours, leisurely wandering through the National Gallery. Apart from the familiar display of Old Masters, I was most impressed by the new interior decorations. Each enormous gallery with ornate ceilings had been recently painted in blue and gold.

As we were leaving, I saw a sign saying "My Queen."

"What is that?" I asked the attendant.

"It is our special Golden Jubilee Exhibition of paintings of Her Majesty, as seen by schoolchildren."

They were wonderful. There were about forty, painted by talented children of all ages and all excellent and so varied. There were two that I shall always remember. One was of the Queen making a cup of tea. The other by an eight year old boy, showed the Queen with about twenty Corgis on leads. The Palace is in the background. On the path behind, where the Queen stood resplendent in her crown, a pile of "doggy-do" with steam arising from it, and the word "POO" in a balloon. Behind this, (very practical) stood a Lady-in-Waiting with a shovel.

By this time we had also been intellectually refreshed and amused. It was time to eat. We enjoyed a meal in a nearby Italian Restaurant before our long walk back over the Wobbly Bridge to Waterloo Station.

Stephen had told me to let him know what train I was catching so that he could meet me at isolated Effingham Station.

"Quickly," said Douglas. "Hurry, you'll just catch this train, give me the card and I'll phone Stephen and let him know you are on the way."

I sat on the packed train. Dusk was slowly forming outside in suburbia. At each station more people alighted until there was only me and a scruffy looking negro left in the carriage. I felt rather worried as I had given the card with Stephen's phone number to Douglas. What if he was not waiting at Effingham? It was now almost dark. The train pulled up at the station, and there to my relief, was an anxious looking Stephen, who greeted me warmly and drove me home as I enthused over my wonderful day in London.

I caught the train to Petersfield another day, where I was met by Rob, Don's cousin and his wife Beryl who made me very welcome in their lovely home. She is a superb cook. We went for a walk to their pretty village, Rowlands Castle.

Stephen lives near Polesden Lacey. I had often passed this large mansion when I lived in Bookham in 1952.

This lovely old Georgian house is where the Queen Mother and King George VI had their honeymoon. Stephen and Alison took me there for a visit. It was a tranquil, sunny day and the setting was perfect. After we had enjoyed a tour of the house we wandered around the gardens and saw the impressive Pet's Cemetery.

That evening I was included in the invitation to his firm's barbecue in a large garden of one of the solicitors in Pirbright. It was all very sophisticated compared with the casual Australian "barbie". There was tennis, mini-golf and badminton for the children. The many tables were covered with tablecloths for the delicious and up-market food.

Stephen and I had to leave early to return to his home and collect my luggage (and fight my way into my compression stockings) then take me to Heathrow for my departure.

This was the end of yet another enjoyable adventure in England.

CHAPTER
FOURTEEN

Two little words 2003

Adventures in the jungle with a three thumbed commentator.
The weather's hot and humid as its so near the equator.

"I'm sorry, I shan't be able to give you massage next Tuesday, I am off to Kuching for a week's holiday," announced my friend Leo.

"Lucky thing, I wish I was coming with you." I replied.

"Why not?" His reply surprised me.

Thoughts and plans flashed through my mind with astonishing speed.

Wherever is Kuching? How far away is it? Is it in China?

I'll never get an opportunity like this again.

Indeed, I echoed Leo's reply in my mind, "Why not?"

I hurried home and mentioned my tentative plans to Don.

"What do you think?" I asked him.

"If that's what you want, it's O.K. with me."

His reply saw me hurrying to the Travel Agent.

"Any chance of booking on the same flight as Leo and staying at the Holiday Inn?" I asked.

There were no problems and I learned that Kuching is in Malaysia, the capital of Sarawak on the western side of Borneo. The population is about 500,000.

"Don't forget the insect repellent." Don reminded me. "You know how the mosquitoes like you."

I was ready for all eventualities with my sunhat, umbrella and anti-diarrhoea tablets, none of which I needed. I always adhere to my old Girl Guide motto — "Be Prepared."

Borneo is the land of head hunters. Don's last words to Leo and me as we left for the airport were: "Don't lose your head!"

The direct flight took five hours with no time change, as it is almost due north of Perth. All year round the climate is hot and humid as it is so near the equator. We only experienced a few brief warm showers during our stay.

Our rooms at the hotel were the standard luxury of a Holiday Inn anywhere, but I found the unique view fascinating.

Immediately below, I could watch various activities on the river and also on the opposite bank. A small ferry constantly plied its ponderous way from shore to shore; rowing boats with earnest crews were urgently training for the imminent regatta; large boats carrying assorted cargo chugged laboriously upstream. On the opposite shore, I spied a Chinaman in a traditional hat sitting immobile, fishing from his tiny craft.

Each day we breakfasted at the hotel. The variety and quality of food we found excellent although they catered mainly for Malaysian tourists. Eggs were plentiful but obviously no bacon in a Muslim country.

Every day I smuggled a couple of buns into my capacious handbag. These with some ridiculously cheap bananas comprised our lunch.

The pattern of our day was to make an early start, breakfast leisurely, then go on a tour. Most days we returned to the hotel to enjoy our smuggled lunch and have a siesta. In the afternoon we explored the immediate vicinity, finding a couple of multi-storey shopping centres adjacent to the hotel; also the ubiquitous McDonalds and Pizza Hut.

Our evening meal we ate with the locals in the clean spacious food halls.

Every one had a hand basin on the wall for the Muslims to wash before eating, an admirable habit.

One evening I ordered ginger chicken and rice, costing only 3.80 ringgits for a generous helping (a mere A $1.50). Everything seemed to be garnished with a fried egg. One lunch time, we sat absorbed, watching two teenagers performing the wearisome task of cutting carrots into fancy shapes, for their parents food stall.

On our first day we took a tour of the city. Most people we met spoke English and were very friendly. Kuching means "City of Cats". During our stay we only glimpsed a few scrawny felines but saw a couple of large rats scuttling along the wide open drains. Statues of cats adorned the city, a few very attractive but most were rather garish.

142

"Oh good, we're going to the Cat Museum."

I had told Leo it was one of my ambitions when we initially studied the brochures.

This modern attractive building stands on a hill and was built in 1993. The comprehensive exhibition covers the beliefs, legends and history and every aspect of cats, worldwide.

Vivid childhood memories of when I was about three, returned when I saw a book displayed called "Furry Friends" with black and white photos of dressed up kittens. I treasured this book for years. Alas, it was probably destroyed in the Blitz. Ancient Egyptian history intrigues me. Anyone killing a cat was put to death. If a cat died a natural death, the owner mourned by shaving their eyebrows. They displayed a grotesque mummified cat circa 3,000 B.C.

Malays believe in the supernatural powers of cats and that it is good luck to keep one. All sorts of ornamental cats were displayed, also cats in music such as "Kitten on the keys" and of course that wonderful musical *Cats*. The philately exhibits displayed all types of cat stamps.

I wished we had time to study all the facets of this unique Museum, but the taxi whipped us away to the impressive Sarawak Museum. There we saw a longhouse complete with tribal artefacts and a large variety of stuffed animals, the taxidermy being superb. The Museum was a combination of local history and natural history. To my relief the labels were in English as well as Malaysian. Later, we also visited an interesting Chinese Museum.

During the afternoons and early evenings, we wandered along the beautifully kept river bank or looked at the shops. Many sold brightly coloured materials for the saris worn by some of the ladies. We recognised a mixture of races, Chinese, Malays and Indians wearing a variety of clothing. Some strict Muslims wore a burka showing only their eyes, others were in colourful dresses or saris and many wore jeans and tee shirts. Everyone looked clean and the children in particular, beautifully dressed and charming. We saw no prams or pushers anywhere, the babies and toddlers being carried, often by their fathers. Prices were very low. I bought a few buttons for the equivalent of two cents each from a shop selling the biggest selection I've ever seen.

The mutilated spelling of familiar words was easily recognisable, such as *bas* for bus and *teksi* for taxi. One morning we took a *bas* for a forty five minutes bumpy drive to the Cultural Village. This very professional scenic park had many of the ethnic groups actually living in the longhouses. The Dyaks who not so long ago head-hunted, gave a very striking dance wearing only colourful loincloths. Heads (or were they replicas?) hung on the walls . . .

We watched demonstrations of beadwork and carvings.

"Oh, look at that dear little girl."

Two women sat on the floor weaving intricate patterns on a loom.

One sang and her daughter, a charming two year old complete with a flower between her teeth, danced and even attempted the traditional hand movements.

Later, a performance in their small theatre showed us the multi-ethnic cultural diversity of this area. The many symbolical dances for marriages, funerals and stories from nature were entrancing. One man demonstrated his expertise with a blowpipe piercing a balloon many metres away. While waiting for our *bas*, some of the performers were waiting for theirs too. They offered us some of the snacks they were obviously enjoying, tiny banana fritters dipped in chilli sauce. I declined the sauce!

One evening we went for a cruise on the Sarawak River and saw a spectacular sunset. As we passed them, large murky crocodiles slid into the river. Then we glided past shanty fishing villages, a sprawling riverside industrial area and the well known Margherita Fort. They told us that this had been named after the wife of Charles Brookes, the first English Rajah of Sarawak. Now it is a Police Museum.

The highlight of our trip was seeing the orang-utans. We met other tourists who had been on a distant jungle tour and seen none. They advised us to visit the Matang Wildlife Centre. The following day we took their advice. This huge enclosed area, about 100 hectares, is for the rehabilitation of endangered wildlife. Their entrance notice pronounced it was for "Recreation, Conservation, Education and Research." Khalik our own private driver and guide collected us from the hotel. A delightful, intelligent young man, he was taking a year out of University to conduct these tours. When we met him, I came to understand literally, the expression "he was all thumbs". Khalik had two on his right hand. They fascinated me but did not handicap ("thumbicap"!) him at all.

This was my first and probably my last visit to a real jungle. It surprised me that it was hilly, for some reason I had always visualised jungle as flat.

"Are there snakes or dangerous creatures?" I asked apprehensively.

"Nothing to worry you," assured Khalik and pointed out a couple of small leeches but nothing more threatening. All the same, I felt the atmosphere was slightly sinister as if we were being watched. I trod on some enormous flat leaves about a metre in diameter and nearly two metres long. I looked up into the dense foliage and was astonished to discover they came from quite a small tree. Huge aviaries housed varieties of eagles and the local distinctive hornbills. These large raucous birds were killed by the locals until quite recently, to use their colourful beaks as a headdress. An enclosure contained some somnolent black sun bears.

"Where are the orang-utans?" I asked anxiously.

"Not very far now," I was told and there they were.

We stood on a platform looking down on three or four of these delightful creatures in an enclosure. Three were engrossed in one corner, eating. A young one cavorted around a central tree stump. This beguiling little ape really played to his audience, frequently checking that we were watching him.

By then, a small group of students had joined us on the platform. After performing various antics, he was joined by a young Sambar deer whose new antlers were still downy. These two, obviously friends, gave us a memorable show. The orang-utan teased the deer, hiding behind the stump. The deer pretended to head-butt him but he darted away. They played like this to the enjoyment of the audience. We realised we had been watching this charming interlude for nearly an hour, an unforgettable experience.

By coincidence we were in Kuching for Festival week. On Saturday, we found it both educational and exciting to stroll along the riverside enjoying the special Expo of Cottage Industries. Local artefacts and foods crammed the diminutive stalls.

"Where is the music coming from?" I asked.

Leo propelled me towards a stage where performances of singing and dancing by well disciplined children made a welcome diversion. We did not stay long as the humidity and oppressive heat had us searching for a drinks stall. Once I ordered a tempting fruit salad and was offered the garnish the locals always enjoyed with it — mayonnaise!

Leo wanted to make two visits that did not particularly enamour me, one to the meat market and one to the fish market. We found there were no longer any meat markets.

Two ambitions of mine Leo patiently agreed to. He sat and read magazines whilst I had a startlingly vigorous reflexology session by a large Malaysian woman. The other request was un-premeditated. On Sunday morning to my surprise and delight we discovered there was a Swap-Meet near the Civic Centre. I bought a striking scarf and a book there. I thoroughly enjoyed the atmosphere of being at a familiar event in an exotic setting.

Chatting to the stallholders and admiring their colourful merchandise, I learned that this was only an annual occasion. How lucky I was to have been there that particular week.

The heat made even strolling in the sun an effort.

"Come on Eve," said Leo. "Let's go to the markets." The ever available "teksi" drove us the short distance. These Sunday markets are for the local people and although interesting, I found them very crowded and noisy. We separated for an hour, Leo indulging in scrutinising the fish market. I wandered around the other very wide-ranging stalls, mingling and jostling with the good natured crowd.

McDonalds, what a welcome sight! I knew this meant as well as a richly deserved ice cream, even more appreciated would be the western style lavatory. My good sense of direction had me return to our designated meeting place on time.

Sarawak is a Muslim country and each morning at dawn I heard the wailing of the muezzin. It is a tribute to their society that with their many diverse religions, Muslims, Hindus, Christians and Buddhists they all live in such harmony. I felt very safe there, probably because crime is punished severely. We saw in one of the daily newspapers that a motor bike had been stolen. This event was actually newsworthy. During the whole of our short visit we saw less than a dozen white people. The whole area seemed as yet unspoiled by tourism.

"Salamat Datang" this message proclaimed "Welcome". We saw it everywhere we went and certainly felt embraced by the warmth (literally) of the country and the people.

We had an uneventful flight home. How pleased I felt to have had the opportunity for such an adventurous holiday in good company, all for reacting to those two initial words of invitation,

"Why not?"

CHAPTER FIFTEEN

Introducing Cornelius

Crocodiles, butterflies, bananas, sugar cane.
Viewing crags and gorges on the Kurunda train.

Cairns is on the opposite side of Australia to Perth. It is
a place I had long wanted to visit although it is
6,000kms away. In May 2003, I decided to book a
ten-day tour with a coach company. They arranged for
me to be collected from home by taxi and taken to the
Airport. Here I met my companions for the tour. We
changed planes at Alice Springs and managed to have a
brief aerial view of Uluru, or what was known as Ayers
Rock. This is the second biggest monolith in the world.

Our brightly painted coach awaited us at Cairns and
took us to our comfortable motel on the outskirts of the
town. The food was excellent, attractively presented,
plentiful and delicious. I put on weight during this
holiday that remained with me as a permanent
reminder of my gluttony. It reminds me of the big bad
wolf in Roald Dahl's Revolting Rhymes.

"I know full well my tummy's bulgin',
But oh, how I enjoy indulgin'!"

After relaxing on the first evening, we had a tour of Cairns the following morning. During a cruise up the inlet in the afternoon, we had some close encounters with some somnolent crocodiles basking on the banks. Their camouflage was so good we had to have them pointed out to us. They resembled statues with evil eyes until one noticed the occasional tail twitch.

The beautiful rolling hills of the Atherton Tablelands enchanted me, so cool and lush and green. To my delight we saw tea plantations but the year's crop had already been harvested. They told us that it took three thousand of the tender young leaves and buds to produce one pound of tea.

I knew Nerada tea was produced in Queensland, but was really surprised when the coach stopped and we were greeted with the delicious aroma of roasting coffee beans. The adjacent factory produced the locally grown coffee.

We passed plantations of bananas and learned about their cultivation. I had no idea that they were not trees and that the stems grew far below the ground. Harvest time loomed and the banana bunches were grotesquely wrapped in plastic for ease of removal.

Driving past these interesting and educational diversions, we passed a large truck that was accidentally dribbling small round objects. I thought they resembled Maltesers, then I wondered if they could be pebbles. To my amazement, I was informed that they were nuts. It must have been a very good crop to fill such a large truck.

151

Another day, we drove past fields and fields of sugar cane that was nearly ready for harvesting. I did not know it could grow up to three metres high. I became aware of how abundantly productive Queensland was, tea, coffee, sugar cane, bananas, and some of the healthiest cattle I had seen.

The road wound past some beautiful deserted beaches until we reached the charming, if rather commercialised Daintree Village. Here we had an interesting trip down the river. We saw cormorants, grebes and even a small brightly coloured kingfisher. The crocodiles were definitely awake, some swimming in the water with only their snouts visible.

The steps on the very wobbly bridge to Mossman Gorge were achieved with some trepidation. I would have been unnerved had I dared to look down. It was well worth it, for the reward of actually walking in a real rainforest. I did not know how dense the undergrowth could be. We were warned not to touch any of the lush overhanging foliage that bordered the path, as many of the plants could be toxic and dangerous. Our guide told us the cautionary tale of a lady who was "caught short" in the forest and used a large convenient leaf in her emergency convenience to wipe her bottom. She developed a fatal toxic reaction. A horrific tail, sorry *tale*!

Travel sickness has plagued me all my life. Fortunately at my retirement, I found some effective tablets to combat coach travel but not alas for boats. The day we visited Green Island, my colour matched its name. We travelled on a packed catamaran on rough seas. It lurched with frightening velocity. What a relief to reach the island.

"Who is going on the submarine?" A voice reached me, as I staggered ashore.

"What does it involve?" I asked with some trepidation.

"We only travel a short distance in a semi-submersible, glass-bottomed craft."

I agreed, as I had the chance of some light refreshment first and felt determined not to miss this opportunity. Sadly the cloudy, blustery weather hid the sun and the vivid colours that I had expected, were absent. We did see a small turtle, some dull coral and a few fish darting about. I had seen a lot more on a television documentary programme.

The spectacular Milaa Milaa falls were worth the long walk to reach them. Framed by the tropical rainforest, they plunged dramatically into the pristine waterhole. I was awestruck. We were told that occasionally, a platypus could be seen but that day we were not in luck.

In complete contrast, we cruised on the calm waters of Lake Barrine, great fun. This large tranquil expanse of water was formed in the crater of an extinct volcano. It is fed by no springs and is purely rainwater. Here we saw a variety of ducks, moorhens, herons and pelicans. Eels and turtles could be recognised in the clear water. Hawks flew overhead and a tame kite swooped to take food from our guide's hand. Returning to shore, we caught sight of scrub turkeys and even glimpsed an amethyst python on the banks of the lake. We visited the famous twin Kauri pines that are reputed to be over 1100 years old then returned via a charming village with an equally charming name — Yungaburra.

Another day we had a spectacular zigzag drive along the coast. (Thank goodness I had taken those travel sickness tablets.) The views of the tropical beaches were stunning. Palm trees framed huge stretches of golden sands. At last we reached the elegant town of Port Douglas. The serene waters of the natural harbour boasted a jam-packed marina.

The beach seemed to disappear into infinity.

"Coffee at the Wildlife Sanctuary?"

"Yes please." We all chorused.

Colourful exotic birds abounded in large well-kept aviaries, many were tame and some to my delight were very talkative. Large enclosures held wallabies, kangaroos, koalas and other native animals. Although I hate spiders, I did appreciate, from a safe distance, the amazingly beautiful Golden Orb spider we were shown.

No sightseeing in Queensland, it seemed to me, could be complete without seeing yet more crocodiles. We zoomed through the rainforest complex in an old army DUKW or "duck" as it is referred to now. This six-wheeled amphibious vehicle travels equally well across land or through the water.

"What does DUKW stand for?" I am renowned for asking awkward questions, but the driver was prepared for this. He explained that the "D" meant it was designed in 1942, "U" that it was a utility vehicle, "K" indicated a front wheel drive and "W" two rear driving wheels. I could never have guessed that code.

The Flecker Botanical Gardens proved to be rather a disappointment. Everything seemed just green; ferns, trees plants and orchids with just an occasional scarlet flower. It must have been the time of the year. All the same I had a feeling of relaxation and serenity there.

The highest point in the area is near Ravenshoe. It had the apt name of Windy Hill.

"Aren't they enormous," I gasped as I gazed up at the huge wind turbines. To the uninitiated like me, the scene resembled something out of a science fiction film. About twenty enormous windmills generate enough power for over three thousand homes in the area.

I had long awaited the exciting day that dawned at last. We were going on the spectacular railway to visit Kurunda. I was not disappointed. The amazing train ride wound its way through dramatic gorges and lush rainforest and I was totally captivated. Later the aerial view entranced me as we descended in the gondola on the famous Skyrail. This is the longest cableway in the world. Below us the forests and ravines were interspersed with countless sparkling waterfalls trickling down the rocky outcrops. I wished time could have stood still.

Kurunda seemed to be a town especially for the tourist. Plenty of shops were dedicated to expensive Australiana and Aboriginal artefacts. Art Galleries abounded with paintings, pottery and sculptures not many to my taste.

Then I saw it, the Butterfly Sanctuary. This is the largest butterfly farm in the world. I have always suffered from a phobia of anything flying around me.

This stems from an unpleasant experience I had with bats when young. I have tried hard to overcome this and can cope with butterflies. I love their variety and radiant colours. My pink blouse attracted them and some large specimens of the local, large, electric blue Ulysses butterflies landed all over me, a bit of an ordeal but I coped. The very informative guide explained some of the differences between moths and butterflies. I knew that butterflies folded their wings when at rest and moths extended theirs. I did not realise that butterflies have club shaped ends to their antennae, but not moths, and that they fly only in the daytime. Lastly she told us that a butterfly's body is small and thin in relation to its wings whereas a moth's is large and plump. They have hemispherical shaped eyes enabling them to see in all directions at the same time.

What a wonderful time we had in this "village in the Rainforest". This exciting day was a fitting climax to a wonderful holiday.

Prior to heading for the Airport on our final day, we visited Barron Gorge. The hydro-electric scheme is underground and we were unable to see it, but the excellent Museum I found very informative.

Our final stop was at the Pier Complex in Cairns where we enjoyed a convivial, delicious lunch. I had spent very little money during the tour, so indulged myself in two very special and treasured items. Firstly, a lovely, Australian made, knitted jacket with intricate designs in pastel shades. This had been reduced from a formidable $545.00 to a still frightening $99.00.

156

Then, passing one of the innumerable souvenir shops, I saw it.

"How much is that crocodile (not doggie!) in the window?" I asked. The middle-aged shop assistant took it out and handed it to me.

"Oh, oh, it is a hand puppet." My delight was obvious as I handed her the money.

"Would you like a bag for it?"

"No thank you, I will carry it on my hand."

It is about a metre long and very realistic looking, rather big to carry surreptitiously on the coach but my seat was near the front. We drove to the Airport for our departure. Imagine the pandemonium I caused as I hid and let it peer over the seat at the passengers, snapping its jaws, a delightful toy, for whom? Me, of course. I called him Cornelius the crocodile.

He is greatly treasured and a perpetual reminder of an enthralling holiday.

CHAPTER
SIXTEEN

A million glow-worms

Meeting family and friends, admiring every view.
A tour of the South Island and Coromandel too.

Since retirement, I have had three lovely New Zealand holidays, the first one was

1997

I set off for this exciting holiday, bags packed with some little gifts for my hosts, and goodbyes said.

I changed planes uneventfully at Sydney and arrived in Auckland about midnight.

David my brother and his wife Dorothy were there to meet me.

They waited and waited. Where was I?

At Customs.

"Have you brought any food into the country?" They asked the routine question.

"No," I assured them.

"Are you sure?"

"Yes."

I am a very law abiding person and would not dream of contravening their sensible restrictions.

"Open your case."

Oh dear, my case had been crammed tight and I was worried that if I opened it, I would never be able to close it again.

They went through my clothing very carefully and came across a couple of gift wrapped parcels.

"What is in there?" The woman asked me aggressively.

"Oh, they are just some wheat bags I made for when one has an ache or pain, a gift for my friends."

I realised as I said it, that I had unwittingly brought wheat (food) into the country.

Fortunately, after confiscating them and giving me a stern warning, I was allowed to go into the Arrival Lounge and meet my anxious relatives.

"Do you know they can jail you for bringing food into the country?"

David greeted me with this scary fact. My innocent face must have spared me that fate.

Next morning David took me to see Bryan Jackson's amazing Museum in Devonport. There was a huge collection of all sorts of items, fascinating.

David and Dorothy were having an extension built to their living area so I was glad not to be in their way for too long.

Joy was my dear friend whom I met in England many years ago. She and George spent a couple of years there with their little girls. For a while he was our local dentist as well as a good friend.

She collected me the following day and took me first across to Murawai to visit their son Glen, then on to her home in Hamilton. She and George had an amicable divorce many years previously.

I spent a couple of happy days there and met Anita and Laurie's little girl Mikaila.

George collected me and took me to his and Marion's new home the other side of town.

We had a pleasant few days together visiting beautiful Hamilton Gardens and nearby Cambridge, a very "English" town full of antique shops.

We also went for a pretty drive to Waitomo Caves. Here in the eerie limestone grottos were millions of glow-worms like stars above us. We were told to keep silent or they would extinguish their lights.

I was returned to Joy where I caught up with her younger daughter Linda.

To my surprise, there was a phone call from David to tell me that our dear cousin Marcelle, in England had died. She was in her nineties and had been a great friend and a real inspiration to me. I felt so very sad and weepy.

Next day, Joy took me to the train at Hamilton Station to meet Gladys, Don's aunt who was already on it, for the start of our exciting tour. It was to include train; down the length of the North Island and across the South too; boat, the ferry from North to South Island, coach, touring the South Island; and plane to return from Christchurch to Auckland.

We had wonderful views of the striking countryside from the observation car all the way to Wellington.

We had a brief tour of the city the following morning in the pouring rain then it was off to the ferry.

I had taken my travel sickness pill as I am a lousy sailor as well as suffering from nausea on coaches. Actually, the crossing to Picton was very smooth, the sun had ventured out by then and three hours later we boarded our coach.

The drive to Christchurch via Blenheim along the coast was unbelievable. Steep hills loomed on one side of us and on the other, calm beaches where fur seals basked. Rivers made exquisite patterns on the landscape below us and everywhere was a luxuriant green.

The weather was kinder now and at Lake Tekapo we visited the Church of the Good Shepherd where over the altar, instead of stained glass windows, we had the stunning view of the lake, God's own art. The water here is a magnificent turquoise due to the glacial waters that feed it.

We also saw the famous statue of the sheepdog, a very necessary assistant to the farmers in this area.

We saw Mount Cook in the distance and the famous Hermitage all nearly obscured by cloud.

Before we arrived at Oaramaru the coach driver asked if anyone could translate for a couple on board who spoke no English. We found out that Gaby and Cécile were French and from then on, we befriended them and I tried to translate basics.

We had driven past the huge Hydro and the lakes of Benmore and Aviemore.

Oaramaru is a big town with some fascinating old limestone buildings. We were told about the little blue penguins down by the harbour but did not see any. The day was dull and overcast becoming more and more foggy, as we headed for Dunedin.

Here it rained non-stop, but it was only living up to its reputation.

A big thrill was the ride on the Taieri Gorge railway an irresistible tourist attraction.

It rumbles through amazing scenery for seventy-seven kilometres, through ten tunnels and over twelve viaducts. Even though the rain pattered on the windows all the way, we were able to appreciate the beauty of the area.

Lanarch Castle, New Zealand's only castle, built in 1871 by William Lanarch for his wife, was an interesting diversion. Very different from an English castle but nonetheless an exquisite miniature replica of luxurious living in the Antipodes.

We then visited Olveston House a local mansion built at the beginning of the twentieth century in a Jacobean style. It was a real insight into Edwardian life in New Zealand.

Gladys was very tired and decided to rest the following afternoon, so I took my umbrella and braved the rain to explore the town.

The schools were finishing for the day and groups of schoolgirls huddled in the arcades in their uniforms. Because of its Scottish links, I had been informed that each school in Dunedin wore a different tartan skirt. Here I was seeing them at first hand.

We left this southernmost city and drove through rolling hills sprinkled with sheep, then the terrain became mountainous.

It is said that sheep in New Zealand outnumber people, sixteen to one.

Lake Te Anau in Fiordland was stunning. We went for a walk along its banks with Gaby and Cécile. I must admit I found the effort of trying to speak French "très fatiguè".

Next day we drove through the long tunnel and very winding road to the boat.

Our trip on Milford Sound fiord to the open sea was very smooth, thank God. The scenery was unbelievable and unique.

We saw large and small waterfalls cascading down the fabulous grandeur of the looming mountains, we even saw seals.

We stopped at the historic former goldmining town of Arrowtown. It oozed cafés and souvenir shops but was fun to browse through.

Queenstown, a very attractive and very touristy town was where I took my two reels of photos in to be developed as we were staying there for a couple of nights. When I collected them they were full of apologies and did not charge me. Their mistake? They had printed them all jumbo size, impossible to put in a normal photo album but nevertheless, they are magnificent, a real bonus.

Gladys did not fancy it, but Gaby, Cécile and I went up in the gondola to the top of the huge hill for the magnificent views and watched folk hang gliding and

163

paragliding. They also had bungy-jumping nearby, pretty scary to see.

This town is nestled on the banks of Lake Wakatipu, another delightful musical name.

We went for a trip on the lake on the vintage steamship that has been plying the lake since 1912, the TSS Earnslaw.

Anyone over eighty travelled free and two of our colleagues qualified.

There was an interesting Motor Museum that fascinated Gaby, but alas, I was not much good at translating technicalities.

Winding our way around more twisting roads we arrived at Haast. The surreal landscape of this area on the edge of the Wilderness was a fitting preliminary to our next stop at Fox Glacier. This glacier and "Franz Josef" are awe-inspiring. A few of the group went over them in a light plane, but I was content to climb up the rocky path and actually stand on a glacier. It was very, very misty and sadly the photos I took were useless.

I was surprised and amazed to see so many pinnacles and crevices in the ice. I believe the glacier moves three metres a day, but imperceptibly.

Greymouth was up the mountain. We had sixty curves in twenty-four kilometres, not for the faint hearted or travel-sickness prone.

Although I had taken my tablets, by the time we arrived there, I felt distinctly queasy.

We admired a very pretty church at Ross, then on to Hokitika. This was a gold mining town, also greenstone was found there. Nowadays, the carving of this attractive greenstone, New Zealand jade, is one of their main industries.

Nearby, we visited Shantytown, a delightful interlude. Here we had a ride on the little train, saw the old forge and hospital, and many tempting jewellery shops.

Then back to grey Greymouth to our hotel. Everything closed at five o'clock and the whole area was empty.

Next day we went to see the Pancake rocks and blowholes at Punakaiki. These stratified formations of the rocks are a dramatic sight. I tried to translate to my French friends but could not think of the word for pancakes, then suddenly, of course, "crêpes". It was disappointing, that none of the blowholes were "blowing".

Back to Greymouth to await our train. We caught the Transalpine Express across the country to Christchurch on the east coast. It took four hours; I have always loved train travel.

We passed through the Southern Alps, spectacular gorges, eventually to the Canterbury plains and lush farmland. The scenery all the way was incredible.

Once in Christchurch, we visited Lyttleton Harbour and then had a long time in the Antarctic Centre.

I went around alone as I am always greedy for information and new experiences, and I had plenty here. It is one of the most interesting places I have ever visited. So many of the exhibits are interactive and the place was teeming with excited groups of children, giving me extra pleasure.

They successfully re-created the environment of Antarctica with a special snow area at −5°C. They even had a wind chill machine for the brave souls who wanted to experience a blizzard at −18°C. There was a replica camp set up and a horde of people who were helpfully answering questions. There was just so much to see and do.

That week happened to be Christchurch's Floral Festival. We went to Victoria Gardens to admire the display.

We stayed very near the beautiful Cathedral but every time I tried to get a good view of it on my camera, there were hordes of Japanese tourists in the square. Christchurch must be a magnet for them.

We went with Gaby and Cécile to the remarkable Botanical Gardens.

There was a mass of colourful flowers and some of the birds that I remembered from England, such as sparrows. Suddenly, the French word *moineau* came to me, to the delight of my new friends.

We saw the Town Crier there as well as some very grotesque statues.

Next day we boarded our plane and said goodbye to our new friends. We exchanged addresses and have corresponded at Christmas each year, always in French, what a challenge.

We had a good flight back to Auckland, then a taxi took us to Gladys's home in Howick.

Next day I had a leisurely browse around the local shops whilst Gladys did essential shopping. That evening we had a pleasant meal with her daughter Carol, husband Martin, and sons Jonathan and Stephen, in nearby Cockle Bay.

We showed them our photos and chatted about the holiday.

I used to baby-sit Carol and her brother Roger when they lived in England.

February 22nd is "Thinking Day" when Girl Guides the world over, think of each other. It is celebrated on that day, as it was the birthdays of both our founders, Lord and Lady Baden-Powell.

Gladys was a member of her local Trefoil Guild. They held a Dawn Service at the top of Viewpoint, a large hill, and watched the sun rise. New Zealand is the first country in the world where the sun rises each day.

That afternoon we went to the Anglican Fair. An excellent Maori choir sang with powerful voices and there were lots of interesting stalls and activities. Later we went to Cockle Bay School where they were having a Mediaeval Fair. Carol's boys were participating in the events.

It was a busy and very happy day.

The following day the weather was dull. In the morning, I accompanied Gladys to the Anglican Church Service. There were seven Baptisms and the atmosphere was very friendly.

Gladys then drove through Mission Bay to the City and the Domain. This lovely park is always a haven of tranquillity. The displays of plants in the glasshouses were magnificent.

On my penultimate day, I went into Howick to look at their excellent second-hand bookshop, always a temptation to me. I succumbed.

We then met David and Dorothy and long time friend Basil, over on holiday from England. We had lunch at a very nice local restaurant and I told them all about the holiday, then we said our goodbyes.

On my final day the weather had turned very hot and humid. I went through my photos with Gladys, and between us we were able to identify where each one was taken.

Gladys drove me to the airport and I thanked her profusely for her hospitality and very congenial company. We were always good friends.

I bought the Duty Free items I always get for Don. We changed planes at Sydney and I was home in Armadale by 9.00pm.

It always surprises me that I suffer from quite a degree of jet lag returning from New Zealand, but I have lost four hours.

What a wonderful adventurous holiday.

2000

I travelled to New Zealand via Sydney again, but this time stopped over and stayed a couple of nights at Kevin's apartment in the city.

He and Carolyn have lived and worked there for some years. He is the eldest son of my English friend Veronica and she happened to be staying with him at the time. Veronica and I had a great time together catching up on family news. As a teenager, I had lived with her Uncle Dan and Auntie Bunny and became part of the family. Veronica and I went to Mass at the church of Blessed Mary McKillop and saw her tomb.

After a light lunch together, I took a taxi to the Airport for the final leg of my journey to Auckland. David met me and I stayed with him one night. Joy collected me the following day.

As usual we drove across to Murawai to see Glen and family, then the long drive to Hamilton. There I was welcomed by her partner, Jerry and J.B, their lovely little dog, (short for "Joy's boy.")

I also stayed a while with George and Marion. We listened to an International Bagpipe competition being held in Hamilton Gardens. Next day we went to Te Aroha Springs. These hot mineral pools are one of the hottest in New Zealand and rich in silica. I wallowed in the 38°C spa. Then, as we picnicked nearby, I got nearly eaten alive by midges.

Back at Joy's I met Anita and her two dear little girls.

Another day I visited the school where Joy was headmistress. The children have various degrees of disabilities and I was most impressed with the care bestowed on them by the staff. This was a real challenge for Joy, and that is what she thrives on.

Joy returned me to David in Milford. Derek, his middle son, was there with his wife Lydia and very shy, delightful little girl Rayna. I have always found Derek to be both charming and empathetic.

The next day David drove me to the other side of Auckland to Don's Aunt Gladys. She was only a year or so older than Don and she and I had always been good friends.

His Uncle Bert's first wife had died and he married Gladys many years his junior. They had a daughter and a son and then immigrated to New Zealand to be near Gladys's sister, who sold them half their block of land. This was a year or so before we emigrated to Australia.

I spent a happy day or two relaxing with her then we prepared for our proposed tour. This time it was to be a short one of the Coromandel Peninsular. We were to be collected from home.

The following morning we were packed and ready early, when Jim, a recently retired policeman, arrived in his comfortable four-wheel drive vehicle.

"Well, you're it." He announced.

"What do you mean?" I asked.

He told us that only seven had booked for this tour, One couple had cancelled, another couple had called in yesterday that they had both been taken ill and we were to pick up one lady in Rotorua.

So, we had a tour with a personal and personable chauffeur who was a knowledgeable and very pleasant host.

Firstly he drove us around Auckland then through Bombay Hills and the very winding road to Tairua. We actually had coffee that day at his home in Coromandel, meeting his partner and lovely cat Fifi.

Two things impressed me in his home. One was the stunning view from his deck across the bay; the other was his real marble lavatory seat. I bet it would be pretty cold in the winter.

We visited the Hot Water beach. Here folk were digging holes and sitting in them. Jim had thoughtfully brought some towels with him and we happily paddled.

In the bush he showed us an enormous kauri tree and also the "lavatory paper" tree. The leaves can be used for that purpose and are also antiseptic.

I was surprised at the size of Coromandel town. We had a ride on Driving Creek Railway through the bush, very exciting. On the top of the hill there were lots of pottery articles and other artefacts for sale.

Next we visited Thames. The gold mine was closing but we were given hard hats and torches and taken under the tunnel, where a man was pushing a trolley full of quartz rocks from the seam above. It was very musty and damp in there.

Waiki had an open cast mine. We had coffee the next day in a superb really old house in Katikati. I love the reiteration in so many of the Maori names.

A big feature of the town was the very artistic paintings on the walls of so many of the buildings.

We passed through Tauranga and saw the lovely beach at Mount Maunganui.

Then Jim took us to Longridge farm. After admiring the pets, we sat on the back of an old truck for a tour of their large and thriving kiwifruit orchard. We were told that the stock lasts a hundred years and are pruned heavily. We admired the very prolific crop.

I also liked the Kumi Kumi pot bellied, black pigs that were very tame. They even sat on command and begged for food like a dog.

At Rotorua our next stop, we collected Pat, a charming English lady on holidays.

The sulphur smell of the area is extremely strong when one first arrives but it is surprising how soon one gets accustomed to it.

We visited a lovely old church with Maori carvings and weaving. There was a large window with an etching of Jesus on the water.

We went to the Whakarewarewa geysers and saw big, intimidating, fiercely bubbling mud pools.

Rainbow Farm was a fascinating destination. Here we saw giant trout swimming in crystal clear pools. They even have a nocturnal house to show off the elusive kiwi.

After a very chilly night, we headed for the East Cape lighthouse. It was a very bumpy drive up an unmade road with rocky, high, crumbly cliffs, very scary.

On to Tolaga Bay and saw its very long wharf as the bay is so shallow. There is a very high Maori population there. The area seemed very rugged and inhospitable.

We then went through spectacular hilly country to the town of Gisborne. We watched logs being loaded and transported by sea to Japan. There was a huge mountain of wood chippings.

The four of us went out for a very pleasant, convivial meal. Jim mellowed with the wine and told us many stories of his policing days.

The peaceful town of Wairoa was on the way to Lake Tutira. Here we walked by the weeping willows and there we saw an enormous caravan, the biggest I have

172

ever seen. It even had room for a small car to drive into the rear of it.

The Art Deco city of Napier gave us a different architectural environment.

Jim took us for an interesting drive through thriving orchards, vineyards and hop growing areas until we saw the peak of Te Mata. It is 400 metres above sea level and we had a terrifying drive to the summit. Once there, it was worth it.

We had panoramic views all around us, magic.

We returned to Napier, then on to Bluff hills for some more spectacular views.

We had a straight through drive to Taupo. Here we watched the Bungy jumping — horrific "sport". The participants were just restrained by their ankles and some dipped in and out of the water, ugh!

Honey Hive, as you would guess, is all about bees and honey. It is a very informative place with a comprehensive shop.

Huka Falls were truly magnificent and attracted many other tourists.

Once again I visited Waitomo Caves and the glow-worms. I am fascinated by the eight-inch long sticky strings of the larvae that they use to trap insects.

It is always very eerie on the boat underground, as the strict silence enveloped one like a blanket.

We had an uneventful drive back to Auckland and were dropped off at Gladys's home in Howick.

My last day, we spent happily reminiscing about our recent adventures and just relaxing.

I packed my case in readiness as the next day, once again I said goodbye to my dear friend as she saw me off at Auckland airport for my flight via Sydney, back to Perth.

Another lovely New Zealand experience.

2003

This holiday was courtesy of Qantas frequent traveller points, as I had qualified for it with all the recent trips I had been on.

Once again I went in February for a few weeks, when the weather is warm and the school holidays over.

I spent a few days with dear brother David and his wife Dorothy in Milford on the North Shore of Auckland. Their lovely home overlooks the sea.

Joy collected me as she usually does and we drove to Hamilton. The following day we returned to Murawai where her son Glen lives, as it was Pat, his mother-in-law's 60th birthday. It was being celebrated with a hangi, a traditional Maori feast. This is a method of cooking in the ground using hot stones with delicious results.

Because Pat's name begins with "P" She decided to have a fancy dress "P" party. There were about ninety guests. Most slept in sheds on the farm or in tents. We were honoured and slept in the house. George and Marion were there but the rest of the people were strangers to me.

It was interesting to see what characters were portrayed in fancy dress.

Glen went as a "pedestrian crossing". His face was blackened and he wore orange stripes. Joy went as a parcel, elaborately wrapped with paper and string and looked most uncomfortable.

Most of the children went as little princesses or pirates. One imaginative man went as a plumber carrying a lavatory! I had gone unprepared, so with a bit of quick thinking, I went as a "Pom".

The following morning, Glen had cooked us a magnificent barbecue breakfast before we headed back to Hamilton.

The next day Joy drove me over to the East Coast across the Matamata Plains to Tauranga, to stay with George and Marion in their new apartment, in a very up-market retirement village.

We went for a fun day, taking a picnic and stopped at the lookout in Quarry Park. One can see a panoramic view over the Bay of Plenty. The gardens were magnificent. We drove through Katikati with its amazing murals.

Suddenly, in the middle of nowhere, I saw a sign "Second-hand Bookshop".

We followed the directions and to my surprise and the delight of us all, there was this large, comprehensive shop. We browsed happily for ages. All sorts of unexpected treasures were within and I found a very good limerick book to add to my collection. The shop was combined with pottery and art sheds.

That evening I was taken to admire the view from Mt Maunganui not far from their home. There were masses of large and small boats in the Marina.

Marion was working the following afternoon so George and I chatted and he showed me his allotment. As they are in an apartment and have no garden, those who wish, can rent an allotment. He had many thriving vegetables growing there.

Before leaving Tauranga I briefly caught up with their younger daughter Linda her husband and their little girl who were visiting. She was idolised by George. Linda had just learned that she was expecting twins, very exciting.

Joy collected me and this time we went directly to her other home in Taupo, not far from the lake. Jerry just adores fishing and happily spends his retirement on his boat.

Back across the country we went the next day, through forests and winding roads to Hastings to celebrate Jerry's mother Jessie's birthday. She lives with her other son John. They had a really beautiful, colourful garden.

Then we drove back to Taupo through the forest again and the hills and steep ravines. The countryside in New Zealand is never dull.

I had said to Joy, "New Zealand has everything. Rain forests, mountains, lakes, rivers, farmland, beautiful beaches, everything except desert."

"You're wrong," she answered. "We do have a desert, I'll take you there tomorrow."

Down along the lakeside, through forests and we were on the desert road. It was not empty sandy desert as in the Sahara but dry, barren wasteland, very bleak.

176

Here is where the army comes for manoeuvres. We saw tanks and soldiers in camouflage. We decided to visit The Queen Elizabeth II Army Museum. I was happily surprised how very interesting I found all their excellent displays. There were comprehensive collections of all types of weapons and also of medals. I happily browsed for an hour or so before we had a light lunch there.

The next day in the pouring rain we returned to Hamilton overnight. I spent the day doing final shopping and of course more chatting.

Before going to the Airport, Joy kindly took me to see Don's Aunt Gladys, my very dear friend.

She was now in a pleasant serviced apartment but sadly, looked very old and frail. She did know me however. I later heard from her daughter that she had been transferred to a Nursing Home and not long after, died. I had rightly guessed it would be the last time I would see her.

I really feel the loss of such a dear and faithful friend.

I was dropped off at the airport for the flight back to Perth. This time it was via Melbourne and quite uneventful.

This short holiday had been a special bonus, affordable one with all my fares covered by my Frequent Flyer points.

Thank you Qantas.

CHAPTER
SEVENTEEN

My right buttock

First I had a car crash, then I had a fall,
My holiday in England was not what I planned at all.

Grandson Simon's birthday in June 2004 saw me leaving home as usual around 11a.m. to visit daughter Carrie and deliver his gift.

I drove onto the far lane of the Albany Highway for a few metres, I indicated turning right on the dual carriageway and was going very slowly when . . . crash . . . I felt the thump of the rear collision.

Suddenly, right in front of me loomed the pale trunk of a large tree. My immediate reaction was to brake. My small car came to a sudden halt right across the two lanes of the oncoming traffic. My guardian angel must have been watching over me. This very busy highway is often full of trucks and heavy vehicles. That morning there was a lull in the traffic. I now know the meaning of the expression "I don't know what hit me".

A young woman had been blithely driving at the specified 70 kilometres per hour, oblivious to my car slowing down and signalling. She was very shattered but not hurt. I sat there dazed. A concerned pedestrian told me to sit still; an ambulance was on its way.

I told him Don was visiting Carrie. He used his mobile phone to contact the ambulance and tell her of the accident.

Half an hour later, Don, the ambulance and the police arrived together. The ambulance drove me a few metres to the hospital where I was assessed, told I had whiplash and sent home.

My neck was sore for some days when lying down, and I had to lift it manually. The three-year-old car was a write-off. Fortunately the other party was covered by insurance and there were witnesses to prove I was not at fault. All the same, it was a very unpleasant, unexpected prelude to my proposed holiday.

The following week I felt well enough to travel to London with Emirates Airline. I had decided to have a couple of days in Dubai to combat jet lag.

June is extremely hot there, but everywhere was air-conditioned. The economy obviously booming, I saw opulent buildings being erected, luxurious hotels, well-dressed people and golden domed mosques glittering in the blazing sun.

I visited an enormous shopping plaza with many international shops. I love people-watching and spent a happy hour having coffee in one of the many cafés.

Stephen, Don's nephew met me at Heathrow after an uneventful flight. We spent the afternoon chatting at his home in Effingham, and I enjoyed a visit to a huge supermarket with him.

179

He and Alison, his partner, are busy solicitors in nearby Woking. She leaves early and returns early. He suffers from his family's dislike of early rising and starts and finishes his day later.

The next day, Alison took me to Woking early where I caught the train to Guildford.

In ten minutes I was alighting in the old county town where I'd lived for many years in my youth. I walked up the steep, ancient, cobbled High Street; I withdrew some money from the Bank and headed for the station. I intended travelling to Hinchley Wood to visit Don's ninety two year old sister. We had always been close friends.

I suffer from swollen ankles but on the plane I had worn compression stockings that had been most effective. This meant that my shoe buckles needed tightening. I intended to do this whilst on the train. Alas, it was not to be. I heard a distinct crack as I fell heavily on to my right elbow. Immediately, two couples were at my side looking most concerned.

"Are you all right?" one asked.

Usually I would say, "Yes, yes," as I hate fuss.

This time I replied, "No, I'm not, I've done something to my shoulder."

"Can you walk?"

I staggered to my feet although my legs felt like jelly. They helped me the short distance to the station where they phoned for an ambulance. A mere three minutes later a paramedic was reassuring me, telling me my shoulder was probably dislocated and could be

180

manipulated. I tried to keep cheerful when I arrived in Casualty, in spite of being in severe pain.

How ironic! We arrived at the Royal Surrey County Hospital where I had done my orthopedic nursing training in 1951. The following year I had a hip operation there. I know I am nostalgic but I had no wish to see the hospital as a patient. The nurse asked me questions.

"Next of kin?"

"My husband Don."

"Address?"

I gave it.

"Oh, he's on holiday in Australia?"

I explained that I was the one on holiday and gave her Stephen's phone number. He dutifully and efficiently became my next of kin.

They X-rayed my elbow that was very bruised and sore but not fractured. Various doctors arrived and tut-tutted over my shoulder X-rays. I nearly passed out with pain when asked to lift my arm. The CT scan gave umpteen more images. After six hours a pleasant doctor approached me.

"I believe you're in England on holiday," he said.

"Yes, my husband's last words were, 'Have a good trip', and I *have*!" I replied with a wry grin.

"My goodness." He was astounded. "I've been in Casualty for five months now and it is the first time I've heard a patient make a joke. I'm afraid we will have to admit you and operate on your badly smashed shoulder."

EVEN MORE ADVENTURES IN RETIREMENT

Before I had left Australia, many friends had wished me well.

> Have a good trip they all told her,
> But Eve would admit she'd grown older,
> So, a "good trip" she had
> And what made her so mad.
> Was she thoroughly shattered her shoulder.

Ewhurst Ward held six beds, the other five being occupied by elderly ladies with broken hips and various degrees of pain and mental deterioration. There was no radio or television but the staff seemed pleasant.

The consultant, Mr Paremain a man about six foot six, concertinaed himself into the chair by my bed.

"I'm afraid that the X-rays show that the head of your humerus is shattered. We could wait until Friday when the shoulder consultant comes but I honestly feel he will suggest a replacement rather than a reconstruction. I could operate tomorrow and give you a cobalt chrome replacement joint."

"Do it," I replied, anything to relieve the pain.

He asked me to sign a form to say I understood I would never be able to lift my right arm more than shoulder height. My signature with my left hand could have been in Arabic!

This was Monday June 21st, the longest day of the year and one I will never forget.

The following day I fasted but was allowed tiny sips of water. Early in the afternoon I was wheeled to Theatre, no pre-med to my surprise. In the ante-room a pleasant Indian doctor gave me what she said was oxygen that smelled of vanilla.

Next thing, I remember someone saying. "Open your eyes, Mrs Day."

I tried to do so. Vaguely I remember being wheeled back to the ward; vaguely I remember the misty figure of Stephen by my bedside. Hours later, I really regained consciousness, to discover I had an oxygen mask, a drip, self-administered morphine and, of course, my arm in a sling. A few hours later I discarded the drip, morphine and oxygen and sat up for a welcome drink.

A few things surprised me about changes in hospital procedures. No one asked my religion, no one was interested in my bowels, very different from the "olden days," with the twice daily enquiry of "Have you been?"

The bedpans were made of disposable fibre. The nurses were surprised but complied when I asked to be called Eve, yet the doctor was Jim to them all. On discharge, when asked the name of my doctor, that was all I could tell them. The ward bathroom was mine alone once I was mobile. No showers were allowed until the clips were removed in three weeks time, they told me. If all is well, then you may fly home.

Stephen, bless his heart, visited me daily around 8p.m. after a long day in his office. "When can I go home?" is the plaintive plea of most patients. Another surprise when they told me I could go when I felt ready. I decided to leave on Saturday, as I knew it would suit Stephen.

The physiotherapist had made sure I could walk up and down stairs. The occupational therapist showed me

183

how to do up a bra with one and a half hands, in the front. Not easy!

During my stay, the sling dragged on my injured neck muscles from the recent car crash. I occasionally undid it. Panic amongst the nurses.

"You *must* keep that arm totally immobile for three weeks."

"Don't worry, I'll hold it in the correct position." I did, but after the anaesthetic I realised to my delight, that I could then lift my head up normally, probably due to the enforced total relaxation.

The costs of this unexpected hospital foray were nil, as Australia and England have a reciprocal health agreement. What a relief!

I had full insurance and phoned the company to tell them of my predicament, my cancelled tour and altered return date.

"Are you flying Business class?" they asked. "I wish!" was my reply.

"Well" said the disembodied voice "You can if you get a letter from the consultant to state it is necessary."

Immediately I phoned Mr Paremain's secretary who assured me the letter would arrive the following day. What a difference to the anxiety of the necessary flight home.

Saturday arrived. Stephen and Alison collected me and somehow had managed to move a bed downstairs. How pathetic I felt. My energy level was nil and I could do very little.

Stephen said his phone bill was paid by the firm and I could phone anyone I liked. I did.

Although I remained feeble for a long time, neither my voice nor my appetite was affected. I had planned to spend one night with dear Maureen and Paddy near Worcester, go on a tour then return to them for a week prior to returning to Australia.

I cancelled the tour, then phoned them with my change of plans and need to return early.

"Oh dear," gasped Maureen. "Whatever's the matter?" Her concern was obvious.

"We knew you would be away that week and I'd already planned a week in Ireland with my sister, who is here from America."

"Oh dear," I re-iterated as I wondered where I could go. Silence.

Then reassurance from my warm, caring friend. "Don't worry Eve, we'll have one day together. Paddy will be here. He will look after you and take you to Birmingham Airport." What a relief!

Now, I had far more important things to think about. One of the big thrills of this holiday was that Emma from Isis Publishing had invited me to lunch on June 22nd. They had published all three of my books in Large Print for the public libraries.

Alas, that had been the day of my operation. Stephen had phoned them and re-arranged the date. He offered to drive me there and was included in the luncheon invitation.

"Eve was off the have lunch with her publisher,
Her ego was ten foot tall.

She'd forgotten the very old adage,
'Pride comes before a fall!' ""

Stephen duly drove me to Oxford where I met the delightful welcoming staff.

I persuaded him to photograph me under the Isis Publishing sign, complete with my arm in the sling.

I chose something easy to eat with my left hand at the lovely riverside pub. I coped reasonably well in the crowded dining room, though feeling far from well.

Suddenly, I was aware of being watched. I looked up and peering at me from the top of the window was a duck. I thought I must be hallucinating. I asked the waitress, "Was that a duck I saw up there?"

"Yes," she laughed. "She decided to build her nest in one of the hanging baskets."

So I wasn't seeing things. I tried unsuccessfully to photograph it. Later I asked Paddy what would happen to the ducklings when they hatched.

"Don't worry," he replied. "They will be able to use their wings immediately and will flutter to the ground."

The following day I spent with long time friend Veronica, who collected me from the neighbouring village. Our jaws ached after a few hours non-stop chatting.

After spending a few days with Stephen, he drove me across country to Essex to stay with dear friends and ex-neighbours Douglas and Margaret, as originally planned. I had phoned them and told them of the accident. They treated me with extra special care.

I even managed to see some of the folk I'd hoped to visit. I coped with tottering around the magnificent Rose Gardens at Rettendon but was easily exhausted.

The problem arose: how could I get across to the west of England to stay with Paddy and Maureen near Worcester? Stephen came to the rescue again. The next Saturday he kindly drove me to Sinton Green, where Paddy and Maureen live.

All Sunday, Maureen and I had uninterrupted quality time together, before she headed for Ireland with Tess the following day. Paddy was so kind and caring the few days I spent with him.

"Michael (his identical twin brother) and Jill have invited us for supper tomorrow, would you like to visit them?" asked Paddy.

"Yes, that would be lovely." I agreed.

It is a source of constant fascination to me, to see two men in their seventies, exactly alike.

They were both employed in the Taxation Department and amongst their many hobbies are music and ornithology. Paddy has also become a keen and knowledgeable odonatologist. What is that? The study of dragonflies. The pond in the woods down their lane has many species that breed there. I love the smells and ambience of English woods.

We had a happy evening with Michael and Jill, singing the old Scout songs.

Paddy and Maureen's doctor is in a charming nearby village. I had dreaded the removal of the clips from the wound on my shoulder, but it was quite painless. The nurse was deeply shocked at the bruising covering the whole arm. Initially very colourful — green, purple and yellow; now it was black. She suggested arnica, which I duly bought the next day. I had a distinct recollection of my mother saying to me as a small child, "Arnica for bruises".

Paddy took me for some short drives and to the beautiful church at Witley and into Worcester.

"Paddy," I asked. "Do you know anyone who will help me put on my support stockings before I fly home?" Fortunately I had coped with personal needs such as washing and dressing although it took a long time.

"Jan-of-the-pigsty will help I'm sure," replied Paddy. An uncomplimentary name for a truly lovely lady who lives near Paddy and Maureen in a charming converted pigsty.

Fortunately Emirates Airlines flew from a number of provincial airports, so I was able to leave from Birmingham, only about an hour away, instead of enduring the hassles of Heathrow. Once my luggage was checked in, I had the humbling experience of being ensconced in a wheelchair. Paddy said goodbye and left me in the tender hands of Jim. He is Veronica's son and my godson. Stratford-upon-Avon where he lives is not far away. We had a long chat for an hour or two, lubricated by frequent coffee.

Departure time arrived and I received priority treatment being in Business Class and in a wheelchair. I appreciated the excellent food and special attention.

Daughter Carrie met me at Perth Airport after our unexpected delay in Dubai.

188

She drove me home to an ecstatic welcome from Bella my little Sheltie.

I think Don was relieved to see me home in one piece after my ordeal. Carrie admitted later how shocked she had been at my appearance and thought I'd aged ten years.

It was not the holiday I had intended. Still I *did* have lunch with my publisher and visited some of my friends. I felt grateful it was not a hip I had broken; at least I could walk and move my forearm. I counted my blessings. After my return, I realised what a lot of caring and supportive friends I was blessed with.

"Oh dear, I can't drive." My plaintive wail was heard by folk from the various groups I belonged to. For four months I gratefully accepted lifts. It was especially frustrating, as my new Mazda awaited me in the carport, an updated replacement of my smashed car.

Some months of intensive physiotherapy gave me only a minimum more movement in my shoulder. I had persisted conscientiously with the painful exercises to little avail. I was able to lift it a little bit forwards and sideways but fear that will be its permanent limitation.

I had to accept that some things would now be impossible. I gave away my easel and massage table. I soon learned to compromise and eventually managed to do more things.

When I first started driving again I needed to lift my right arm on to the steering wheel with my left hand. Later, I discovered that an easier way was to swing my body and arm around to reach it.

At last I was driving again and normal life could once again be resumed after my "adventure", well . . . almost.

Dressing myself took ages and new techniques were adopted. Showering was a pleasure being under the water, but oh, the painful and difficult ordeal of drying myself. This was and still is, very time consuming and awkward — my right arm movement being severely restricted. How can one dry one's right buttock? With difficulty!

Hence, the title of this chapter!

CHAPTER
EIGHTEEN

Surprise at the Tattoo
2005

Mars bars in church and a surprise at the Tattoo.
The Great Wall, Summer Palace and ancient Chinese loo.

After my disastrous holiday in 2004, I decided to indulge myself the following year.

If there is one place in the world I would really like to explore, it is Great Britain.

> A painter who came from Great Britain
> Hailed a lady who sat with her knitain
> He remarked with a sigh,
> "That park bench — well I
> Just painted it, right where you're sitain."

I saw very little of it when I lived there, due to various circumstances: lack of opportunity, lack of finance, lack of a vehicle plus the responsibility of a family.

Saga Tours Australia had sent me a tempting brochure three years in succession.

In 2005 I succumbed.

It was called the Three Universities Tour of Britain and involved staying in the student's rooms all with en suites, during their vacation. All food and tours were included in the price and we would not need to handle our baggage. This was a big selling point for me as I was still very limited in my abilities after the accident to my shoulder in 2004.

The tour operators were in Melbourne, and we were to fly Air China with an option of four days in Beijing on the return journey at a very reasonable extra cost.

It all sounded very exciting and just what I wanted.

I found it almost impossible to contact John, the organiser, but when I did he was always very reassuring about any queries.

I discovered later from the many Melburnians on the tour, that he had fobbed them off with all sorts of excuses.

Unfortunately Air China does not fly from Perth, so I had to spend a night in a hotel in Melbourne and leave a day earlier.

We left at 6.30a.m. for a ten and a half hour flight and stopped in Sydney and Guangzhou. The huge, stark airport at Beijing was far from welcoming and just seething with people. No one spoke or understood English, only our guide when we eventually found him. We were left for a long time in the foyer of our overnight hotel whilst rooms were sorted out.

Some of us found our luggage had been damaged, to our consternation. The padlocks on mine had been gouged open but I did not find anything missing, (or added.)

I had insisted that I have a single room which, of course, was obvious in England in the student's rooms. Here, I had to share. Fortunately, it was with a pleasant Scottish lady who did not snore.

Our nine hour flight to Heathrow was ghastly. The food was inedible, the announcements unintelligible, and the attendants totally surly and indifferent. They did not even check our safety belts were on for arrival.

90% of the passengers were Chinese, all very smartly dressed.

I will not elaborate on the conditions in the unusable lavatories, with open buckets for soiled sanitary towels. Ugh!

"Thank God we're nearly there," A welcome English voice was heard a few rows behind me. I saw a couple of Western faces. I saw them again when we arrived at Heathrow and realised they were on our tour.

We collected our cases and awaited the Saga coach.

Our cheerful Cockney driver Matt drove us to our first venue, Writtle Agricultural College, University of Essex. Holly our tour guide accompanied him.

A delicious supper and a warm welcome awaited us, and then we were shown to our comfortable but rather austere rooms.

I had particularly asked for a downstairs room as I was still nervous of falling after my accident. I was put upstairs.

"Never mind," Holly assured me. "I'll make sure you are on the ground floor next week."

It was great to be able to unpack and know that this would be "home" for the next seven days.

The following morning in the spacious dining room I was happily bewildered by the vast choice of dishes for breakfast. There were huge bowls of grapefruit, my favourite — peaches, cereals, yoghurts, croissants, toast, various rolls, plus eggs, bacon, sausages, beans, hash browns, and various juices, tea and coffee too.

I really made a pig of myself the first few days but ate more sensibly as the days went by.

Each morning as we boarded the coach we were handed a small bag. As soon as I was seated, I investigated it.

"Swap you my ham and salad sandwich for an egg and cress?"

I said each day, as I craved for my childhood favourite. As well as the sandwiches, we had juice, yoghurt, cake and a piece of fruit daily.

Our first visit was to Cambridge. I had been there briefly as a very small child but could remember very little. I was longing to wander through the ancient colleges and just soak up the atmosphere of this famous city.

A Guide boarded the coach and our first stop, for far too long, was some way outside the city. Here we reluctantly visited the U.S. War Cemetery. None of us were Americans.

We did divert on the way back to see Grantchester, the village made famous in Rupert Brooke's poem

"Oh God to see the branches stir,
Across the moon at Grantchester —

194

— Stands the church clock at ten to three
And is there honey still for tea?"

I felt disappointed that the clock was not fixed at that hour permanently.

A piece of trivia that we were told is that Jeffrey Archer, the then infamous author, lived in the lovely old vicarage.

At last we arrived back in Cambridge for a few hours exploration, all carrying our lunch bags. My priority was to eat and dispose of mine, so I found the delightful Market Square and sat on a bench enjoying the ambience of this great city.

I wandered through some of the side streets and found the Archaeological Museum.

It was huge and fascinating but I had to ration my time there, which was just as well as it was invaded by a huge influx of Japanese tourists.

"Could you please tell me where the Ladies Room is?" I asked an attendant.

"The door opposite the top of those stairs." He told me.

I stumped up the steep flight of stairs and opened the door to a real delight of a "Museum piece" lavatory. It was in a very large, high room with an old fashioned hand basin opposite an equally old W.C. with the sort of cistern and chain I remembered from my childhood days, not quite an archaeological find, but very apt in such a venue.

I strolled around the grounds of Pembroke and another College, and then found the fascinating

Fitzwilliam Museum. This is a treasure trove of art and artefacts, but by now I felt very weary and was glad to avail myself of their charming tearooms and Museum shop.

I browsed for a while before enjoying a well-earned pot of tea.

I then roamed through many of the galleries and in particular, appreciated some of the lovely old books and manuscripts as well as a cornucopia of famous paintings.

I found my way to the meeting place by the pub on the river bank, where punts awaited to take visitors out, complete with young men in their traditional boaters.

Each evening after dinner, there was optional entertainment for about an hour.

We had a talk on the area at each venue which was very helpful. The local Barbershop Quartet, quizzes, dancing displays and even a one-man "Music Hall". Jim, a talented, versatile entertainer sang many of the songs I remembered from my childhood.

Next day we drove to the County Town of Colchester, Essex.

I was stunned by the exquisite, colourful floral shows in most of the towns we visited. Apparently, there was a competition running in England for the town with the most beautiful floral display.

The castle grounds were unbelievable, brilliant beds of all types of flowers, a floral peacock and clock and also the cannons. I had not realised their significance. One cannon was said to be the original Humpty

Dumpty that defended Colchester during the English Civil war in 1648.

I had planned to see places rather than people, who are usually my priority but I did make a couple of exceptions.

Writtle is a charming village mentioned in the Domesday Book in 1086.

It is complete with Tudor houses, old pubs and a village green with duck pond. I found the pargetting fascinating. Many centuries ago, designs had been stamped on wet plaster to decorate the outside of many of the village houses.

My Melbourne friends were amazed that I had never visited this area when I was in Essex, as it was only about ten miles from Wickford where we had lived before immigrating to Australia in 1969. In those days we had a young family, no car, and limited finance, so did not travel.

I decided to opt out of the Sunday outing to Southend. The day was very wet and turned out to be rather a non-event, apparently.

Whilst in the area, I caught up with a few of my old friends and neighbours including Don's brother.

He and Sally had visited us in Australia once and had talked about their home. He said he had a 60 foot bedroom, I could not believe it until I saw it. David is a very successful commercial artist and designer, and runs his business from his home in Suffolk.

The building was a converted 16th century barn and the whole of the top floor was their bedroom, it included their dressing rooms and a pleasant office, and yes, it *was* 60 foot long. The whole place was mind boggling.

We visited Gainsborough's house in the old town of Sudbury. It was in the market here that I bought a couple of expanding watch bands big enough for my large wrists, an unusual memento.

We stopped at our last Essex venue at the grand country mansion of Audley End. We only had limited time and I remember eating my lunch sitting on a bench in the drizzle, admiring the sopping wet gardens.

We then crossed to the west of England on the coach to Reaseheath Agricultural College, not far from the ancient and picturesque town of Nantwich.

Again, to my dismay I was put in an upstairs bedroom but one kind lady offered to change with me.

I loved the rural setting. Each day the black and white cows passed my window on the way for milking. The lake and the colourful herbaceous borders were a joy.

Our first outing was a day in the Peak District National Park. Unfortunately the weather was dull but we enjoyed the drive through the Derbyshire Dales and visiting small towns all with grey stone buildings to match the skies.

Old churchyards fascinate me and in the one in Hartington I saw some very sad tombstones where families had lost numerous very young children.

We went to an interesting cheese shop. I had forgotten we were in Cheshire and that this was also the home of the famous Stilton cheese.

198

Next day the unrelenting drizzle continued, but it did not deter us from visiting Little Moreton Hall. This is a really quaint, large, old, Tudor, timber framed house. It was irregularly shaped and over 500 years old. Our Guide there was most entertaining.

The visit to the Wedgwood factory was to be one of the highlights of the holiday and turned out to be one of the most disappointing. Bad management had us visiting there on a Saturday when all the manufacturing plant was dormant so we had a boring tour of uninteresting machines.

I did enjoy the optional film and the coffee in the cafeteria, using of course Wedgwood cups. The price of even the "seconds" in the elegant shop, was prohibitive.

On Sunday, those who were interested were taken by the College bus to the beautiful old 14th century of St Mary's in Nantwich.

It happened to be the children's service and the vicar was talking about the miracle of the loaves and fishes. He called four of the children by name and gave them each a large Mars bar. He then sent them off with the verger to see if they too could perform a miracle.

They re-appeared at the end of the service with sheepish grins on their faces and hands behind their backs

"Well?" asked the vicar "Have you performed a miracle?"

"Yes," they chorused, producing plates of Mars crackles made by mixing the bars with Rice Krispies.

199

After the service, we all retired to the church hall for tea or coffee and to enjoy the fruits of the children's labours, a delightful interlude.

Another free day we enjoyed visiting the Market Square where local people brought fruit, vegetables and other items for sale.

Off we went to Wales the next day, to Erddig House. (pronounced Erthig)

I was bewildered with so much to see. There was the house itself, crammed with many unique artefacts and the attractive gardens.

There were also two signposts that had me trying hard to decide my priorities. One said "Second-hand books" the other, "to the Art Exhibition".

I went to the Art Exhibition first. Rod Williams had a charming display of water colours on a variety of subjects. At the time, I was his only visitor and we had a long chat, even promising to send each other original Christmas cards.

The bookshop too, was a pleasant surprise and of course, I bought a couple of books.

Before leaving Cheshire, we had an outing to the wonderful, historic, county town of Chester. Sadly, it was another wet day but we were not deterred.

I spent a long time exploring the vast Cathedral and enjoyed a coffee in the original old refectory. There were a lot of Roman tombstones in the intriguing museum but a piece of trivia that appealed to me, was the tombstone of a 19th century woman, who had 33 children, including 15 sets of twins, whew!

Strathclyde University, right in the city of Glasgow, was our last venue in Britain, definitely an urban environment.

> There was a young girl of Strathclyde,
> Who ate sour apples and died.
> The apples fermented
> Inside the lamented,
> Made cider inside 'er inside.

Our first tour was to the enchanting Burrell Collection, a comprehensive display of artefacts and art, a mixture of Art Gallery and a Museum and quite fascinating.

Another day we had an all too short cruise on Loch Lomond. The black clouds loomed over us so we headed back for the shore and got there just in time, before a violent thunderstorm had the boat rocking alarmingly.

We went on the ferry to the Isle of Bute, spending a few hours in Rothesay. We visited a huge, rather vulgar, Victorian Gothic mansion, Mount Stuart. I was more inspired by the area's local "Gents" of the same era.

This was open to visitors and had been beautifully renovated. I took a photo of our driver Matt discreetly posing there.

On our itinerary we were to spend a day visiting the Falkirk Wheel. I was not particularly looking forward to it, until I saw it.

This was Scotland's magnificent Millenium Project.

It linked two canals with water levels 115 feet apart that once needed eleven locks and took all day. Now it can lift 600 tonnes of water over 25 metres in four minutes. The massive and elegant steel structure uses minimum energy. Each turn of the wheel uses less than eight boiling kettles, what a comparison!

This masterpiece of engineering was a surprise and delight for me who had not anticipated it.

On the Sunday, our free day, I caught up with Roger and June who live in one of the outer suburbs of Glasgow. I had met them some years before, when Maureen, Paddy and I stayed with them for a memorable few days.

Roger writes me long letters each Christmas and always asks when are they going to see me?

During this tour, I was able to spend a day with them and their beautifully mannered little grandson.

They took me to Hill House at Helensburgh not far from Glasgow, the original home of the publishers of many children's books, Blackie's. I remembered "Blackie's Annuals" and many of their books. The building and everything in it, even the window catches, were designed by the renowned artist, Charles Rennie Mackintosh. The whole place seemed so modern, I found it hard to realise it was designed in 1902.

We all went to the tearooms there and had some of the most scrumptious scones I have ever eaten.

When I told Roger that our final treat for the holiday was the visit to the Edinburgh Tattoo the following evening, he was most envious. He and June had been many times but they would have liked to have taken young Brodie.

"Its useless," Roger told me. "We locals don't stand a chance of getting tickets; they all go to the travel agents."

That evening during our meal in the University dining room, Holly asked me if I was going to the Tattoo.

"Of course," I answered.

"Isn't everyone? I thought it was to be the highlight of the tour."

"No," she replied.

"Some of them have been before, and we will have had a busy day and they want an early night as we leave on Monday at 3.00a.m. for the long coach drive to Heathrow."

So I was able to get three spare tickets for Roger who was delighted.

I had a brief reunion with them the following evening at the Tattoo.

"Ladies and gentlemen," said the announcer. "It is a lovely evening, although it is a bit chilly. We have people here from all over the world, but first I would like to give a very special welcome to Eve Day of Armadale, Western Australia."

I could not believe my ears, was I hallucinating? Yes, he did make that announcement. I saw the big grin on Roger's face and knew the perpetrator.

It was the biggest surprise I have ever had.

A few hours later after we had returned to the University, at 3.00am we were off on the long uneventful drive to London along the Motorway. It seemed quite unnecessary for us to have left so early as we had a very tedious seven hours wait at Heathrow for our Air China flight to Beijing.

Only about eleven of us were going straight there, the others were either extending their tour in London or visiting relatives.

Beijing Airport was again a nightmare, seething with people, and no-one seemed able to speak or understand English. It took us one and a half hours to get through passport control.

Our very good guide Sam, who spoke adequate English, accompanied us on the hour's drive to our hotel.

Everything was very ornate there and some of the notices did have an English translation. One that amused me was in the Coffee shop.

A large sign proclaiming that they sold "Milk Sharks"!

Again, we found that only a minimum of staff spoke a minimum of English.

Next day we ventured out in the mini-bus.

Beijing was wet, polluted and very grey, both the buildings and the skies. We headed for the Forbidden City passing Tiananmen Square.

It was massive and can hold over a thousand people but what impressed me, was the long, patient queue of families on school holidays, all waiting to file past Mao Zedong's tomb.

The weather was oppressively hot, humid and smoggy with intermittent downpours, not a good time to be climbing up and down endless steps but it was worth it.

The Forbidden City was the Chinese Imperial Palace from the Ming Dynasty to the Qing Dynasty, and took over one million men fifteen years to build.

Yellow is the colour of the Emperor (I don't think they refer to his skin!) and most roofs are this colour. The outer city walls are 6 metres deep and 7.9 metres high. For added security there is a 52 metre wide moat.

Each wall has a gate in it and there is an ornamental tower on each corner. Some of the Palaces had lovely names such as the Palace of Heavenly Purity and the Palace of Supreme Harmony.

Afterwards, we visited the very ornate Summer Palace with its gardens dominated by the lake and bridges. One had 500 lions engraved on it. We saw the impressive Marble Boat too.

By now we were feeling inundated with so much information.

On the way back to the hotel Sam pointed out some signs in a street and told us that they meant "massage".

"Have any of you had Chinese massage?" he asked, "Velly good".

A couple of men on the tour sniggered but I was seriously interested.

I would not have ventured into a side street but I had seen massage advertised in the hotel in their "health rooms" on the lower ground floor.

I booked myself in for one having no idea what would transpire.

One stays fully clothed for this massage. Lui Yong, a lithe, very strong young man gave me the most intense massage I have ever had. It lasted about 75 minutes

205

and was reasonably priced. He must have spent nearly half that time on my face and head.

He then lifted my left arm and powerfully massaged every muscle there. I got panicky, my right arm is unable to be lifted now and I did not want him to force it. He spoke no English so I had to rely on signs.

I undid my blouse at the top (I hope he did not think I was trying to seduce him!!) and pointed to the still livid scar on my shoulder, raised my left arm then pointed to this and shook my head. Message received and understood.

I then relaxed and enjoyed this amazingly beneficial experience.

On Saturday we went for an acutely uncomfortable rickshaw ride through the side alleys of the old city. Most accommodation for the huge population is in the ugly high rise buildings, but a few of the original hutongs remain in the alleys.

The first we visited was an old people's complex around a small courtyard.

An 83 year old man with good English, so rare in Beijing then, told us how happy he was there. Traditionally, the children care for their parents but he said his daughter was too busy. He showed us his meagrely furnished room with little more in it than a bed and a large television. He ate communally and on the bare wooden shelf he had rows of pills and little else.

In contrast we then visited Mr Wong, a prosperous middle-class business man.

His home encompassed two sides of a courtyard. By Chinese standards it was quite luxurious but we found it to be very basic. The interpreter helped with explanations. In a row of tiny bamboo cages were his pets, each cage held a small cricket.

We then visited the Drum and Bell Tower, a huge rather grim building dating back to 1210.

No clocks or watches then so the time was broadcast to the people of Beijing by bells and drums.

Inside we enjoyed the traditional tea ceremony, again with the help of our interpreter. I had developed a real taste for Jasmine tea and I bought myself a "magic" mug from their shop. They had demonstrated them and I am a sucker for gadgets. The picture on the outside changes to a totally different one when hot liquid is poured into it.

The small bowl of tea and now this one had me pretty desperate for a lavatory.

This was one thing I had dreaded about this holiday, having to use the traditional squatting position that the Orientals use. Up until then, I had coped waiting for a "western" one at tourist venues.

Now I had no choice. I scuttled off in the direction I was told. It may have been the "Gents" but I was beyond caring. I managed to squat alright but had a terrible job getting up again with nothing to aid me. Still, it was an experience!

We had asked Sam to take us to some Markets but he deposited us at the Sun Dong An Plaza, an enormous multi-storey building selling mainly clothes. Like everywhere else, it seethed with people.

Eventually I found a McDonalds and bought a welcome ice cream, as the building was stifling with little or no air conditioning. I bought some sweets that resemble little stones too, similar to ones I had bought in Europe.

Afterwards I went to a Pharmacy opposite to get some tweezers, as I bought a pair of excellent ones years ago in Hong Kong.

What a fiasco.

Of course no one spoke English. I tried to show them what I wanted by sign language. The man kept pointing his finger upwards. I hoped it was not a rude sign.

I then saw a flight of stairs and went up them. They kept offering me scissors until I finally managed to convey my needs. The tweezers were not much good, but again, it was an experience!

The following day was to be the big event I had long looked forward to, the visit to the Great Wall.

We set off in teeming rain that did not abate all day.

On the way there, we were deposited for ages in a huge jade factory. I suppose they hoped we tourists would be big spenders. Similarly, we were taken to an interesting, prohibitively expensive, silk factory on another occasion. They were doomed to disappointment there too. All the same, the life-cycle of the silkworm has always interested me and some of the articles were very beautiful, but not to my taste.

I was most surprised to find we were driving through large peach orchards on the way to the Ming tombs.

The first tomb was the most impressive as it was set up as a Museum.

208

Two colourfully dressed soldiers guarded the entrance.

Only two tombs were open to the public both dating from the 15th century although altogether, there are thirteen.

I was entranced by the large granite statues of both people and animals lining the pathway.

After lunch, we finally arrived at the Great Wall.

The rain made visibility almost nil.

All I could see was a myriad of umbrellas as I pushed my way through the hordes of people, past the souvenir stalls and managed to stagger up some of the uneven steps to the second stage of the Wall.

That was as far as I got but I did see a misty tower in the distance and took a very indistinct photo before descending and hurrying back to the mini-bus.

That was the sum total of my visit to the Great Wall of China.

That evening we visited a theatre to see a group of acrobats from the Provinces give an amazing and highly disciplined performance.

It had been a very busy, interesting and tiring day.

We said our goodbyes to Sam the next day at Beijing Airport as we queued for our departure to Melbourne.

Somehow I got separated from the others and was desperate to find a lavatory. I dared not leave the queue and my large suitcase.

The girl sat hunched at her desk periodically yawning and tapping half-heartedly on a computer.

The queue did not move.

A pleasant Chinese business man behind me, who spoke English, became very agitated and annoyed at the delay.

It was good to have a personal interpreter. First we were told that the baggage belt had broken. Then there was a delay due to "misfortune" whatever that was. It took one and a half hours before my case was processed.

By now, I was in a terrifying state with my bladder but could see no signs of a lavatory.

I was brusquely directed to "Immigration" and all I wanted was "Departures".

I could see none of my fellow travellers, only a mass of Chinese people.

Tears welled in my eyes out of worry and desperation.

An extremely tall Chinese official, who spoke broken English, saw me and ushered me through an adjacent door straight into the Melbourne departure lounge. There were my other tourist companions and to my relief, literally, the welcome lavatory.

A short delay on the plane and an inedible meal, and we were in Shanghai for a brief stop, or so we thought.

We returned to the plane and waited and waited.

Eventually we were told, "Take hand luggage and return to Airport."

We all stood with our hand luggage and waited and waited.

Then we were told, "All return to seats."

We duly obeyed. Another half an hour and once again we were told, "Take hand luggage, return to Airport."

By then, I and probably everyone, was totally exhausted. I could not possibly have staggered up the long flight of stairs with my hand luggage.

Joyce had the only wheelchair. She, Beryl and I were ushered along an endless corridor into a huge empty room, completely desolate.

The attendant pointed to the lavatory signs and water fountain, and there we were left for two hours.

I was now desperately thirsty and nearly went for some water then remembered the rule. "Never drink unboiled water in China".

Joyce and Beryl slept, I tried to read, I was glad I had brought my water bottle with me, it still contained a little.

I thought I might even cope with the stairs when the attendant returned and took us in turns in a small lift to join the other very disgruntled tour members.

Why had they not shown us the lift initially?

An explanation for the delay was "Problem with battery charger".

This sounded ludicrous to me, imagining the small gadget I use at home for my torch batteries! Apparently, it was of serious concern.

When I told my nephew who is an Air New Zealand pilot that I was travelling Air China, he pulled a dreadful face.

"Oh dear," I said. "Are they that bad?"

He tried to reassure me by saying they had a good safety record, so I kept remembering that during all these uncomfortable hours.

There was absolutely nothing open in this vast barn of an airport, not even a coffee shop.

We were brought cans of some revolting liquid, and attractive boxes containing some very weird inedible items. I did bravely try what might have been cake.

We had been grounded for a long six hours before resuming our flight to Melbourne. Many of the passengers were very upset as they were missing ongoing flights.

I have two dear friends in Melbourne. They had intended meeting me and spending a few hours at the airport with me until my flight to Perth at 3.00pm so I was not panicking.

We had been due in at 6.30a.m. and arrived at 12.30p.m. I never expected Muriel and Gaye to be there but how delighted I was to see their smiling faces.

We had time for an elongated coffee and chat before I boarded the welcome Qantas plane for Perth.

How I appreciated the environment, food and helpful staff who actually spoke English.

What a day! And what a holiday!

CHAPTER
NINETEEN

Collections, computers and compulsions

Massages and Church Retreats, collecting this and that.
Pornography and making cards and donning my red hat.

Over the years I have attended classes on a variety of subjects but one I really enjoyed and continued to use was massage. I had a portable table complete with a face-hole and occasionally took it on visits to massage people.

I also learned the potent therapies of Reflexology and Reiki but have never had much opportunity to practise these. I attended a monthly massage workshop locally. A small group of us practised various techniques, massaging each other. Two people massaging one person is the ultimate bliss.

Basically I am lazy. I have never been athletic or competitive and have to discipline myself to exercise. Even whilst I was still working, I attended exercise classes for the over 55s. This minimum age was later raised to 60. They are run by a Physiotherapist from

Royal Perth Hospital. We have a mixture of exercises, balance, muscle-stretching and strengthening.

A few years ago I also joined the Armadale Mall Walkers who meet twice a week. We are a group of people sponsored by the Injury Control Council of W.A. Starting early in the morning at 7.35a.m. before the shops open we walk laps of the local shopping mall.

This has many advantages. It is safe, flat, air-conditioned, seats are available and of course lavatories too. We have company and chat as we each go at our own pace and we can go shopping afterwards. We often indulge in that much needed cup of coffee.

For some years, I have belonged to the Kelmscott Writer's Group aptly named "Come Write In." We have had a core of stable members and many others have joined us for a while, which brings a breath of fresh air to the group.

These men and women often have many talents they were unaware of, until they started putting pen to paper. (Some writer I am, using these clichés!) Each year, we have published a small collection of our works and reading them, one sees what diverse backgrounds we come from and what a huge variety of subjects we have written about, in both poetry and prose.

A big part of my life, now that I am retired, can be spent in socialising and keeping in touch with my many friends and acquaintances. Various groups I have been connected with or old colleagues will meet regularly for lunch at a local venue. This is one of the many joys of retirement.

The women's fellowship group at our local church, the Majellans, was sadly disbanded a few years ago as there was no longer a need for stay-at-home mothers to have outside contact. Nowadays so many playgroups flourish and many mothers are working.

Majellan retreats have been held twice a year at Safety Bay and with one exception when we were moving house, I have attended them all. They have been led by a variety of nuns, priests and lay people. I find it is an island to escape to where I can find refreshment, physical, emotional and spiritual.

Saturday evenings there are a time for some fun.

On occasions I have read the group some of Roald Dahl's Revolting Rhymes. I have gradually collected basic props and "dress-ups" to dramatise them. We had great fun with Red Riding Hood, also the Three Little Pigs, using the masks I had bought in Canberra. One year I remember casting our President who was just five foot tall, as the giant in Jack and the Beanstalk. She was ecstatic. The cast mime spontaneously to my reading and they and the audience have a great time and many laughs. Good for the soul!

I have also used the same method with the Probus Committee at their Christmas lunch one year.

I think the best show was when the U.3.A. Committee dressed up and David wore the mob cap, glasses and shawl as grandma!

My involvement with the church diminished when I decided to no longer be a lector. I had read in St Francis Xavier's church for over 35 years but could no longer lift the missal due to the limitations of my replacement shoulder.

I have happily continued to be involved with the St Vincent de Paul Conference, attending fortnightly meetings and going out weekly to visit local people who are in need. This could mean anything from assistance with power bills, procuring essential furniture and clothing but most often the need is for food vouchers.

We never go alone and over the years I have had a number of congenial partners.

In 1999 "Small Christian Communities" (S.C.C.) started in Armadale. We are a very large and scattered parish. The idea was that small clusters of parishioners who live in the same vicinity, should meet fortnightly for spiritual refreshment, communication and of course, physical refreshment too. I have been involved in one such group since its inception.

I was never very good at drawing so it came as a pleasant surprise to find I had a small amount of talent when dealing with colour.

Water colours were fun and a challenge but it was the instant results of pastels that delighted me most. I did a pastel picture of our cat for Don's eightieth birthday. I then felt sad we had not one of Bella so I did one of her too, both from photos.

It was a fiasco trying to get a photo of "Min". Every time she was posing, she yawned. I have enjoyed experimenting with all sorts of other media too.

I continue to be a compulsive card maker for the pure pleasure of accomplishing a small useful article. I have used ribbons, rubber stamps, punches and coloured sands. The quick and easy encaustic wax is a favourite. Once I get motivated I find this hobby happily addictive.

If only I had learned to type. How I regret it now. Writing has been a hobby for a long time but only since retirement have I tackled anything as ambitious as a book. I can hardly believe that this is my fourth. My others were typed by a friend whom I paid. This time I have risen to the challenge and am typing it myself, very ambitious.

That brings me to yet another hobby/interest I have developed recently, learning the mysteries of the computer.

Over the last few years I have attended some beginners' classes but I feel it comes down to three basic rules:

1. Learn to switch it on.
2. Learn to switch it off.
3. Don't be frightened of it.

I have slowly gained some knowledge by experimenting and using email. This is a great way to stay in touch with friends all over the world. Gradually my familiarity with the keyboard has improved. I have only recently discovered the wonders of the "Net". Any query has an instant answer.

There is so much more for me to learn and I have the rest of my life to do it in.

Oliver, a computer "whiz-kid" from very young, would have been proud of my attempts.

I have continued my interest in Swap Meets and garage sales but am now very strict with myself and limit what I buy.

A year or so ago I went to a local garage sale. It was a very sad situation. The middle-aged American woman's Austrian partner had very recently died. As well as grieving, she had to sell everything quickly as she was returning to America.

"What is for sale?" I asked.

"Everything." was her reply.

She was seated at a nearly new computer with a large, flat monitor.

"Is the computer for sale?" I asked.

"Yes," and she told me the very reasonable price. "But you can't have it until the 16th, the day before I leave, as I use it each day to contact my family."

I think that is all she used it for.

I left a deposit and duly collected it on the appointed day and brought it home.

I managed to connect it to my printer and get it to work, all by myself. I checked where all the plugs had been and was delighted with my independence.

It has an excellent sound system which I have not yet fully appreciated.

I saw some programmes were already on there and I logged on. What a shock!

Oskar, her partner had a huge collection of pornography! Not child pornography, thank God, very much *adult* porn. The poor man must have turned in his grave knowing a stranger was watching his collection! His partner possibly was unaware of the content of the programmes.

I had a belated, explicit sex education. There were men and women, threesomes, men and men, women and women and many of these were actually videos. Whew! My eyes were popping out of my head and my hair must have been standing on end. An innocent sounding title such as "Rose's Garden" gave me a shock when I checked it. I will not expand on the goings-on in Rose's garden! I managed to delete all his carefully researched and treasured items that doubtless had given him much pleasure.

The computer was still under warranty and was a good buy in spite of the initial shock.

Years ago, I remember reading the poem by Jenny Joseph that has now become famous about wearing purple with a red hat when one gets older. The theme is that as one ages, one cares less for convention and can do things just for the sake of fun. I could not agree more.

There was a group of laughing ladies at the next table in a local restaurant last year, all dressed in their red hats/purple clothes regalia. They each wore a name badge with an outrageous name such as "Princess Cutie Carol". I chatted to one of them and she told me they had three "chapters" in their area. She spoke with an English accent, so I asked with a grin.

"What, you dare to wear red hats?"

"That's our secret!" she replied laughing.

In England there used to be a saying: "Red hat, no knickers!"

The idea of the Red Hat Clubs caught on and now there are over a million members world-wide. The rules? One must wear purple and a red hat — that is all. Each chapter is autonomous and arranges a programme of fun activities. Ours is a small, intimate group and called "Women of Spirit". I am still rather new but have been welcomed by the other "Hatters". I did not presume to be a princess, so my title is "The Right Honourable Adamant Eve".

Last Christmas we went to Perth to a big department store, to visit Father Christmas.

We have had a teddy bears picnic with teddies dressed appropriately and a visit to the Art Gallery to name a few of our activities. There are no committees or meetings, just fun.

For years I have been a compulsive collector of all sorts of things, some unconventional. Don made me a mirrored, double wall shelf from jarrah for my sizeable collection of ginger jars. Some were really beautiful. Alas, I had no room for them when we made our final move but fortunately Marion and Carl wanted them and they now reside in their new home. I just kept a couple out of sentimentality.

Amongst the many, many books we have, I have a modest (if that is the right word!) collection of books on the history, geography and humour of lavatories.

I also collect books on limericks, my favourite form of rhyme.

I have a great collection of all sorts of kaleidoscopes. They dwell in a small glass display cabinet, all except one. Last year I visited a local fête. A man had a stall there selling fine-looking wooden articles and toys that he had made. I thought the large cylindrical object on display was a telescope until he invited me to look through it.

"It's a *kaleidoscope*," I said delightedly. With trepidation, I asked him the price.

"It is not for sale," he said "It is being raffled and drawn today."

I had one ten dollar note left in my purse. I spent it all on raffle tickets. To my amazement and great delight, I won this magnificent article. It now sits proudly on a tea trolley with a small lamp adjacent to illuminate the colours as one turns one of the two large cylinders. It is made from beautiful rich jarrah, similar to mahogany and is a treasure for posterity, as well as being my pride and joy.

When my eldest daughter Marion was a teenager she started to keep a record of all the books she read. I have followed her example and for many years I not only record what I have read and by whom, but I also grade each book from one to ten. I find I read about half fiction and half non-fiction. I have always loved autobiographies, but perversely rarely enjoy novels written in the first person.

A favourite author of mine is Bill Bryson. He came to Perth a few years ago to promote his book "Down Under". I had a pile of his books with me for him to sign.

"Gee," he said "You must be a fan of mine."

"Oh I *am*," I gasped. "Do you think I might take a photo of you signing them?"

"Sure," he said.

The very affable assistant suggested:

"How about a photo of the two of you together?"

He put his arm around my shoulder as we smiled at the camera. I could hardly believe it. Did I ever wash that shoulder again?

CHAPTER
TWENTY

Write now

This is how I wrote my books and when and where and why.
I hope the narrative appeals and they're not dull or dry.

Words are the clothes that thoughts and experience wear.

Part 1

I always remember this quotation from Rudyard Kipling that I heard when I was very young.

> "I keep six honest serving men,
> (They taught me all I knew.)
> Their names are What and Why and When
> And How and Where and Who."

These were his aids when writing but also in learning about life. I shall use them as a loose guide to explain how I wrote these books of my memories.

223

What?

Initially, I intended to only write about the very fragmented memories of my very fragmented childhood. My grandparents, only one of whom I hazily remember, had fascinating backgrounds.

How many devout (but not bigoted) Catholics can boast a rabbi for a grandfather or another who was Corsetière to King Edward VII?

I intended to record, hopefully with a bit of humour, the varied and different people with whom I lived and the very many diverse schools that I attended.

This first book, *Adamant Eve*, sees me coping with life from a pampered early childhood with a nanny and a cook, to possessing one small suitcase and having no permanent abode.

Bombing and the London Blitz were vivid memories as was my mother's untimely death that had been kept a secret from me.

I had requests from folk to know what happened next, so I wrote *EVEntful Years*.

This covers the years between leaving school and getting married.

I had a variety of careers (and boyfriends) and some exciting activities.

Post-war England was changing, as the economic position improved.

These years were far from dull.

"Complete the Trilogy." I was urged. A few years had passed and I decided to do just that, after so many people had asked me to.

EVEntually, intended to be my final book, is as long as the other two together. It should be, as it covers forty years of my life in forty chapters from marriage to retirement.

Here I relate many amusing incidents concerning our children and of life when we had no phone or car and considered that normal!

Then came the big adventure of emigration and all that it entailed. Our life in Australia, now nearly forty years, has not been uneventful. The narrative of so many incidents in our new lifestyle was recorded with nostalgia and pleasure.

Now, here I am, unexpectedly telling of the many activities and holidays I have enjoyed since retiring.

My life has never been dull or boring but then I would not allow it to be.

This is the book that is very much an afterthought but I hope will be enjoyed by those who asked me to write it.

Why?

Initially I think the catalyst was Oliver's death. He had always wanted me to record my childhood.

The books are a light hearted, historical documentation of my life, well, the parts I wish people to know about!

I wrote them —

- for my own satisfaction,
- hopefully for the enjoyment of others.

- Certainly not to make money. I had not long retired and had enough money to self-publish, an expensive exercise.

I have always thought of myself as a very ordinary person with limited capabilities. It never occurred to me that my childhood and background were so unusual. My early years were fragmented and often traumatic, but I also looked back on many happy incidents. Thank God for a sense of humour. I think I have been haunted all my life by some of my childhood experiences.

The joy of writing one's own memories is that one can choose what to write and what to omit. If nothing else, the exercise of stretching my memory back over seventy years has helped me to lay many ghosts.

When?

Half way through 1998, I decided to discipline myself and actually start writing. Once started, I felt a compulsion to finish each story.

Although I was retired, I found I was extremely busy and involved in many activities but I have discovered I can always find time for anything I really want to do.

Ninety per cent of my writing has been done between 5 and 8a.m. but not for long stretches. I probably snatch half an hour or an hour when I can. One reason that I chose that time, is that I like solitude with no interruptions.

After the euphoria of the first book launch and initial sales, I thought that was that, then people who had read *Adamant Eve* kept asking me

"What happened next?"

It had never occurred to me to write a second book. At the time, I was attending the Kelmscott Writers Group and used this discipline with encouragement from the group, to write the whole of *EVEntful Years* chronologically.

Another few years elapsed and folk started asking

"When are you completing the trilogy?"

Once I felt the inclination to write again, I found I was much more relaxed about it and was actually enjoying myself. People were still not satisfied and pestered me

"When are you writing your next book?"

"When I've been retired ten years." I procrastinated. I am ashamed to admit it is nearly thirteen years now since retirement, but at last, I have made the effort.

How?

I certainly did not sit at a computer and write as my thoughts materialised.

This would have been ideal, as one can then expand, alter and correct.

Only with this volume have I been computer literate enough to tackle "going it alone".

How I regret now never having learned to type. We did not have the opportunity to learn at school and I knew I did not want to work in an office, (although ultimately I did).

I had read and enjoyed the books by Faith Addis of the humorous accounts of her family and adventures. I contacted her publisher and wrote to her.

Her intriguing titles such as *The year of the cornflake* and *Green behind the ears.* inspired me to have "punny" titles for *my* books but her real inspiration came from the fact that when I met this delightful lady, she told me she had written all her books in ball-point pen and paid to have them typed. So, I could write my stories after all.

A right handed writer named Wright
In writing "Write" always wrote "rite",
When he meant to write "write",
If he'd written "write" right,
Wright would not have wrought rot writing "rite".

So how did I write? In an exercise book in pencil initially: I then used a ball-point pen to write legibly on foolscap paper to give to my typist friend.

In this book, I have cut out a lot of the work, as I struggle to produce the final article from the pencilled notes. Each book has been written by a different method.

My childhood memories are just that. No diaries or records but a lot of unexpected photos of these early years and particularly the evocative recollection of smells. Most of the people I lived with and their characters are indelibly printed in my memory.

228

I wrote each chapter as isolated incidents and had quite a bit of difficulty assembling all these stories into a coherent order for the book. I was eventually satisfied with the sequence.

David, my only surviving brother was amazed when he read *Adamant Eve*. He is nearly seven years older than me and his upbringing was quite different from mine. He had no idea of the traumas and insecurity I experienced and of the many happy times too. Children are very resilient.

EVEntful Years I wrote chronologically, from the day I left school until my wedding day. I still retain vivid memories of those days in Guildford when I had little money but a lot of fun. I value the various occupations, boyfriends, relations and friendships of those years that helped me to expand my limited horizons and grow up.

We thought all the old family photo albums that my mother had so lovingly produced, had been lost in the Blitz. It was a very exciting day when they were found in Aunt Ella's home along with some of mother's diaries. These inspired me to start keeping one, if only a cursory entry:

"Took baby to clinic today, did washing, raining, so hung it in conservatory."

Hardly exciting, all the same, I had a record of daily events and at the back of each diary I would often jot down some of the amusing sayings of the children. I am so glad I did, as they can so easily be forgotten and

I was able to incorporate them into stories in the book.

EVEntually was written most definitely with facts, as I could refer to these diaries as a great aid to memory. I have a friend Kath, who lives in a suburb with the delightful name of "Innaloo". She has had articles published and I valued her expert advice.

As soon as I had completed a couple of chapters we would meet in the coffee lounge of the Alexander Library in central Perth. Here, over endless cups of coffee, she would return the edited chapters with advice and suggestions.

She told me that people who write autobiographies, often suffer from "I" disease. In my case I had "was" disease. It is incredibly difficult to write about the past and not use that word constantly.

In each successive book she found less to correct — I was learning.

I knew I did not want to write a sterile recital of events, such as —

"I was born in —". I decided to just record a series of incidents, hopefully with a bit of humour.

Where?

The answer to this is in one sentence. I sat in the sitting room, in a comfortable chair, with a beanbag tray on my lap, a good light and wrote.

Who?

Who was writing about whom? I wrote about the many experiences and people who have touched my life in various ways or influenced me. I am definitely a "people" person. They are always my priority in life, be it a relative, friend or child.

I have included many powerful characters in these books such as Uncle Harry who played such a vital role in my life.

Another "who" is *who* bought the books, so I shall expand on that, so varied and unusual were the interested buyers.

Part 2

"I happen to have one on me." That has been the real secret of trying to sell copies of my books. My handbag had to get bigger and bigger, until it held three books. I needed to always keep a set or two in the car.

I had no idea what was involved in formatting a book. So many decisions to be made, what type and size of print, where the photos are to be placed, colour and design of the cover, even whether the page numbers should be at the top or the bottom of the page.

Jenny who did the formatting was a charming and helpful lady. She asked me if I was having a book launch.

"What is a book launch?" I asked her, never having been to one.

"You need a venue, some drinks and nibbles, a supply of your books and someone who will say something nice about you," she answered.

So I "launched" my books. On each occasion, I chose a Saturday afternoon and was allowed to use our Parish Centre. Friend Kath, my patient editor, kindly offered to give the introduction.

I then invited lots of people from the many groups I was involved in and was delighted to see about forty people each time. I had tried to whet their curiosity in the little talk I gave and must have succeeded, as everyone (or couple) who came, bought a copy. That was a very encouraging start.

I am blessed with a few good friends but also many, many acquaintances and had lived and worked in the same area for over thirty years.

If I had sold the books through a shop, by the time they had taken their commission, the price would have been exorbitant which was why they have all been sold privately with one exception.

I was cheeky enough to send a copy of *Adamant Eve* to Isis Publishing in Oxford, England, as I had read many of their Large Print autobiographies.

It took them a while to respond, but when I received the reply, I think it was the most exciting moment of my life.

They actually asked me if they could pay me for the exclusive rights to publish the book in Large Print for distribution to libraries throughout the English speaking world. I could hardly believe it! I really *was* an author.

232

I have told of the big thrill I got actually visiting Isis Publishing and being taken out to lunch by Emma in 2004.

As each book was completed I forwarded it to them and each time the wait for acceptance was less, so eventually, they actually published all three books.

Another big thrill I got recently was when I was reading another Large Print autobiography. The page opened with: "Also available in this series".

Suddenly, I saw two of my books included on the list. There was my name and the titles of the books in print, what a surprise.

Another exciting day was when I saw my book in one of the local Charity shops for sale.

It was being re-cycled, I felt as if I'd really arrived.

Before going to be published locally, there were a lot of technicalities I had to learn about. Firstly, I had to apply for an ISBN number. All published books require this.

I also discovered it was obligatory to send a book to the National Library in Canberra and The Battye Library in Perth.

Many of the groups I belonged to were most encouraging and not only attended the book launch but also kindly bought copies.

Some of these were the Probus Club, local branch of U.3.A, Older Women's Network, Trefoil Guild, the Retreat I attend twice a year, St Vincent de Paul members, Parishioners, Keep Fit Group and of course my colleagues in the "Come Write In" Writers Group.

Someone at the Contact Lunch asked me about the book and our speaker Kay Hallahan bought one. My financial advisor bought one when I was talking about the book launch.

I have sold books to my hairdresser; the owner of the craft shop where I replenished my rubber stamps and even the travel agent at Thomas Cooks when I was booking a holiday. I have sold a number when I have been on tours and weigh my luggage down with them, hopefully. I rarely return with any.

Quite a few of the mothers of my old Pre-School children have bought them. In one instance one bought three copies of each book to give as Christmas presents to her "children" who were now adults!

I sat on the train next to a friend who was asking about the book. I had one on me and showed it to her. She bought it and we were chatting about it.

When I alighted, a complete stranger confessed she had been eavesdropping and was very interested in the books. She bought three copies that I delivered to her husband's workshop.

On another occasion, I had gone to a Garage Sale and bought a number of fascinating old postcards. When I got home to gloat over them, I found they included some personal photos, a wedding and a death certificate.

I returned them and said:

"I saw some cards from Shalford in Surrey. I lived there for a while. Who do you know who sent you these cards?"

"It was my sister," She told me.

I mentioned that Shalford featured in *EVEntful Years* and she was most interested and bought one of each of the copies of the books. There I was at a Garage Sale and ended up selling to the sellers!

Over the years I have been asked to give a couple of talks on writing books. The best title I was given as a subject was to a Probus Club. I was asked to talk on: "Everyone has a story to tell." How true!

I am proud to say that at least four people I have heard of, have now started to record their memories. I stressed that I am no academic and there are no rules. Also, one does not have to publish, just get the facts down in writing.

I spoke to the Achievers Club in Citiplace and gave a talk at our local library that was very well attended but I don't like giving talks.

I have never minded reading aloud, but speaking in front of an audience makes me extremely nervous and I worry myself sick beforehand. It is usually alright on the day!

At all these talks I have been fortunate enough to sell a few books.

My books have been bought by various people who have sent them to a number of countries including New Zealand, England, Canada, U.S.A, Switzerland, France, Singapore, and I even heard at one of the book launches, that one was in Mongolia. At that news, someone took a photo of me with my mouth wide open in surprise.

Surprise is the main emotion I have felt over actually writing and successfully publishing these books.

It proves:

- It is never too late to learn.
- You don't know what you can do, until you try.

I have a little motto on the wall of my study that I have tried to live by: "Failure will never overcome me if my determination to succeed is strong enough."

CHAPTER
TWENTY-ONE

A Moving Experience
2006

Decisions made, we want to move. We have the
house for sale. It sells.
We move to our new home. We needed to down-scale.

Years ago, in my forties, I had an occasion to visit a lady in the Dale Cottages complex just across the highway from where we lived at the time. These modest, compact retirement houses were close to amenities and would need minimum maintenance, but they were very tiny. I remember thinking that I could never live in one until I was at least sixty. They say that "old" is fifteen years more than one's present age. I fully agree.

Many, many years passed and only Don and I were living in the house we had moved to in 1992. It was a good sized home which we loved in the suburb of Mount Nasura, part of Armadale. One thing I particularly appreciated, were the number of floor to ceiling cupboards throughout the house. By 2005, all forty four feet of them were full to capacity.

A few of my friends were moving to units or retirement villages but initially I dismissed the thought. We still had our cherished little dog and cat.

Our home was suffering from neglect. The oven door didn't shut. Cracks were appearing on the walls, the original wallpaper that had been there for twenty five years, looked decidedly jaded and dated. The house needed a general face-lift.

The garden too was suffering. Don loves to grow things but the quarter of an acre was too much for him to cope with.

Since the accident with my shoulder, when I could no longer lift my right arm, I too, was limited in my abilities. Soon after that accident, sadly, our little dog died.

In 2005, we heard that Dale Cottages were demolishing eighteen of their small cottages with big gardens and replacing them with larger cottages with small gardens.

The plans delighted me. There were two double bedrooms and a small study, well fitted kitchen and bathroom, two lavatories, large laundry, and a reasonably sized sitting and dining room. They even have a very generous, thirty seven power points in this small house. What more could one ask for?

I was particularly pleased with the size, as Don and I have had separate bedrooms for many years.

> The marital life of a man and his wife,
> This pattern quite often assumes.

First two in a bed, then each in a bed,
Then each in separate rooms!

We had put our names on the long waiting list. But the worry was, whether we would be high enough on the list to qualify for one of these new cottages. The other problem was, whether Don would actually agree to move, he does not like change.

My friend Dawn has a similar cottage built a few years ago and allowed us to visit it and question her. Don was quite impressed.

Then, early in 2006 the great day arrived when we were told we had qualified for one of them. There were three designs, some were duplex some were detached, all of them acceptable. The detached ones had already been taken when we applied, but near the end of the year's wait, we were informed that Sheila had decided not to move, and her detached cottage with one of the larger gardens was available, just what we wanted. The garden is even large enough to have a full sized shed.

We decided to put our house on the market early in the year which in retrospect turned out to be a wise move, as the market for housing was good during those months. What an effort it was, to try and keep the place reasonably clean and tidy for prospective buyers to view.

We had a very patient, capable, enthusiastic Real Estate agent. Whilst we were trying to sell the house, Don was rushed to hospital with a very nasty condition, pharyngeal dysphasia. This made him unable to swallow any liquids as they went straight to his lungs and caused pneumonia. He was unable to eat and could only swallow puréed foods and thickened drinks that were like slime, poor man. The specialist decided it was a virus that time alone would heal and he very slowly recovered. He was in hospital for ten days and returned very frail and listless.

Meanwhile, at least the house was smoke-free when prospective buyers called.

A few months after we had put it on the market, a couple bought it as an investment, which is what we had hoped for. They were most pleasant to deal with and happily allowed us to rent it from them, until our new home was completed. What a relief to have that hurdle over.

The huge ordeal of sorting a lifetime's collection of possessions then followed.

I have no one to blame but myself for the enormous accumulation in all the cupboards. I went through them slowly and systematically, sorting things into four piles;

- things to sell
- things to give away
- things to keep and
- rubbish.

I remembered the old adage:

> When you move, if in doubt,
> Take it with you, *then* throw it out."

Built into the dining room wall, was a lovely glass cabinet full of knick knacks. A few were precious or of sentimental value, these I placed on the top shelf to keep. I then invited family and a few special friends to choose an item as a memento and gift from me.

I had three garage sales and carted endless loads of "stuff" to the local St Vincent de Paul charity shop. We still had boxes and boxes to take. I love the convenience and size of banana boxes. I accumulated about sixty and labelled them all.

I spent a great deal of time measuring the furniture and working out on squared paper, exactly where everything would go. Most of our furniture would fit comfortably into our new home. We just had two wall units and a few minor things to dispose of.

Don had reservations about moving. Where would we put all our books? We had over two thousand. We had a rebounder that Don used daily, a bulky item, where would that go? What about his cumbersome hi-fi equipment? Lastly, but by no means least, what about the cat?

We were told "No pets", but had heard that a few people had elderly cats. "Min" was thirteen. We decided to smuggle her into the house, although I think it is public knowledge that we have her. We told her that she was there illegally and not to let anyone see her. When the doorbell rings, our "secret" cat hides under the bed.

> We have an intelligent cat
> Who refuses to hunt mouse or rat.
> She'll just lie in wait

> For food on her plate,
> Now who could blame her for that?

Some of our books are in the wall unit in the sitting room. The others are in a variety of bookcases with which we have lined one wall of the large integral garage. This room is a joy to me, with its "magic" remote control door, so very convenient.

Mac built a cabinet for Don's hi-fi, but he rarely uses it, not so the rebounder, (an individual superior trampoline). As soon as we moved, we obtained permission to have a sturdy covered patio erected at the rear of the house; there it resides, to be used by Don daily.

These cottages are not freehold, but "Lease for life". All structural improvements we want, such as an extra rail in the shower, need permission. We have pleasant, willing maintenance staff, who will do anything, from fixing the rail to even changing a light globe.

The front door mat is recessed and we have a spacious hallway and extra wide bathroom and lavatory access. The whole place is wheelchair friendly. (Heaven forbid!)

Gillian gave us a house-warming present of an attractive, pictorial, ceramic plaque. Just for fun, we have it by the front door with the name of the house, "Day's End" written on it. This is an ordinary residential road with houses opposite us. It has recently been converted to a cul-de-sac.

I had not been aware of the size of the Dale Cottages Complex. There are more than one hundred and seventy dwellings. There is also an excellent Frail Aged Hostel and a Nursing Home. Our neighbours are very pleasant. Buses, trains and the new large shopping centre are all within walking distance but sadly, the walk is not flat.

Moving day arrived and to my relief, everything fitted where I hoped it would.

We had put some large cupboards in the garage as well as the bookcases. There was also a generous built-in store cupboard at the rear that we had shelved. Here I stacked about forty of the labelled boxes.

Initially, the garage became the dumping ground for all sorts of paraphernalia.

The car remained outside for most of the summer as there was no room for it inside. I slowly sorted out all the articles and boxes and gave myself the self-imposed deadline of Easter to complete it. I made it, just.

We decided to pave the back garden and have over thirty feet of raised flower beds by the fence and wall. It did not take Don long to have thriving roses in these beds. We have a variety of pots filled with flowering and foliage plants there, and on the patio, and hanging baskets too. We even have a square patch for vegetables. There is plenty to keep Don busy as he loves gardening.

I never envisaged moving into a retirement village but I just love it here, now we have settled in.

I live in hope that like the end of all good stories, we will "live happily ever after".

Accept the changes that age brings but stay young inside.